5/98

D0565617

COACHING OFFENSIVE BACKS

Steve Axman

COACHES CHOICE™

ISBN: 1-57167-088-2

Book Layout: Andrea Garrett
Diagrams: Andrea Garrett
Cover Design: Deborah M. Bellaire
Text Photos: Bill Pegram and Ryan McKee
Cover Photos: Sean Openshaw/Arizona Daily Sun (front cover)
                Sports Information Office/NAU (back cover)

Coaches Choice Books is an imprint of: Sagamore Publishing, Inc.
                                          P.O. Box 647
                                          Champaign, IL 61824-0647
                                          (800) 327-5557
                                          (217) 359-5940
                                          Fax: (217) 359-5975
                                          Web Site: http//www.sagamorepub.com

DEDICATION

To my wife, Marie, and our four daughters—Mary Beth, Jaclyn, Melissa and Kimberly.

ACKNOWLEDGMENTS

Much of the material in this book was taught to me by Homer Smith, former Head Football Coach at the United States Military Academy at West Point. Homer is a great teacher from whom I have learned much. I am extremely grateful to him for having given me the tremendous opportunity to have coached at West Point. Very special acknowledgment goes to the memory of West Point's former Offensive Coordinator and close friend Bruce Tarbox, with whom it was my good fortune to have been able to coach for two years. Bruce was a great coach in the truest sense of the word. He aided my career enormously.

Thanks go to the memory of Army passing game Coach Mike Mikolayunas for his assistance with parts of the book. Special thanks to my Northern Arizona Lumberjack football players Brian Galbraith, Travis Brown and Kevin Stephens for their help in posing for the demonstrative photos.

The author is also grateful for the efforts of the staff at Sagamore Publishing, Inc. for making this book a reality. The author would also like to thank Roseanne Cowles and Dr. Cedric Bryant for their proofreading and editorial assistance respectively.

CONTENTS

PREFACE

In my 22 years of coaching football at the collegiate level, I've had the opportunity to work with a number of outstanding young men. In the process, I've observed that a critical factor in the level of success that many of these players were able to achieve was their ability to perform the various skills and techniques attendant to their position in a mechanically sound and consistent way. Perhaps, no position requires more attention to detail than the offensive back. Not surprisingly, the margin between those quarterbacks and running backs who achieve a relatively high level of success and those with comparable talent but who fail for whatever reason to play up to their natural abilities is often relatively slim. In my opinion, proper coaching plays a major role in ensuring that every player plays up to his abilities.

I wrote this book to provide coaches at all competitive levels a tool that can enable them to explain to their offensive backs precisely what to do and how to do it on the playing field. *Coaching Offensive Backs* offers step-by-step instruction on how to perform the basic techniques and fundamentals involved in offensive back play. The book features chapters on ball-handling skills, center-to-quarterback and quarterback-to-ballcarrier exchange techniques, quarterback passing techniques, offensive back receiving techniques, ball security, and offensive back blocking techniques.

I sincerely believe that every coach can benefit from the information and methods presented in this book. If you're a coach who wants to get the most out of your team, *Coaching Offensive Backs* can help you reach your goal.

Steve Axman

CENTER-TO-QUARTERBACK EXCHANGE TECHNIQUES

Every football play starts with the center-to-quarterback ball exchange. You don't want to start a football play with a timing miscue or fumble. If you do, you may rob yourself of a scoring opportunity. At best, you will only lose a down. You can demoralize your entire team and make your job of moving the football much more difficult. It's easier to do it right the first time than to try to recover from disaster. Secure center-to-quarterback exchange techniques give you the best possible chance for success on each play.

The center-to-quarterback exchange should be practiced every day in a variety of game-like situations with many repetitions, in order to make the exchange automatic and fail-safe in all game conditions. Centers and quarterbacks should repeatedly rehearse quick-count snaps, the "goosing" technique, snapping a wet ball, and other situations likely to occur in a game to ensure consistent and sound center-to-quarterback exchanges for all situations.

CENTER-QUARTERBACK STANCES

Every play starts from the center's normal blocking stance. The center must grip the ball in such a way that it reaches the quarterback's hands in the laces-up position for the quarterback's passing grip. Usually, the center begins with his right thumb slightly in front of the first crossing lace.

The quarterback assumes a nearly flat-footed stance, but with his heels slightly off the ground. Since too wide a stance causes false or hitch stepping, his feet should be slightly less than shoulder width apart. He should stand as tall as possible, head up, chest out, so he can best see and study the defense. Visibility of the entire field is crucial. Slight toe-to-instep staggering of the feet can be utilized. However, such staggering of the feet must always be consistent as to the left foot or right foot being up. Staggering the feet is a way to eliminate false stepping.

The quarterback should stand close enough to the center to allow a comfortable bend in his arms. He must, by no means, be straight-armed and tense. The comfortable bend in his arms will allow the quarterback to initiate his movement back from the center while keeping his hands in position to receive the ball.

The quarterback's hands are positioned under the center, with the middle finger of the top hand pressing tightly along the seam of the center's pants. The fingers are spread and extended but not rigid. The bottom hand thrusts down and back at approximately a 135-degree angle, starting with the thumb being placed with the knuckle in between the knuckle and the base of the thumb of the top hand.

9

The bottom hand's fingers are also spread and extended but not rigid. The bottom hand also attempts to press the top hand up into the seam of the center's pants. Although the center's snap technique attempts to split the "V" of the quarterback's hands, the bottom hand is in position to stop the ball, even if it is snapped poorly and is pushed too far to the left. The quarterback's hand positioning is shown in Figure 1-1.

Figure 1-1
Quarterback hand positioning.

THE CENTER SNAP AND QUARTERBACK RECEPTION

The controlling concept behind the center-to-quarterback exchange is for the center to split the "V," the junction between the quarterback's hands. The center should think of the motion of the ball as a straight-line pumping action from the ground straight back and up to the wedge of the quarterback's hands. As he brings the ball back, he should cock his wrist so the ball arrives in position for the quarterback's passing grip. The center does not swing the ball back in rigid-armed pendulum fashion, but flexes his elbow, enabling a straight-line path to the "V" of the quarterback's hands. He also does not lift the ball to the top hand. The center attempts to split the wedge, striking the heels of both of the quarterback's hands with equal force. The idea is to try to drive the ball through the "V," assuring a firm, consistent, reliable delivery of the ball. The center's snapping action is shown in Diagram 1-1.

Another aspect of the center's technique is to attempt to skid the ball off his own left buttock as he pumps the ball into the wedge of the quarterback's hands. This allows him to deliver the ball with the right end slightly elevated (refer to Diagram 1-2). This skidding action off the center's left buttock also helps prevent the pendulum-style delivery. The aiming point is just to the left of the seam of the center's pants and helps bring the ball correctly into the quarterback's hands. The slight upward tilt to the right also matches the quarterback's hand position better.

The center must be sure that he does not lift his tail up as he snaps the ball. He should move forward, keeping his back and tail level. The center's job is to deliver the ball properly. The quarterback's job is to apply constant pressure against the seam of the center's pants and to give the center a fixed target.

Pump back in a straight line to break the heels of the QB's hands

Don't swing the ball up in a pendulum-type of straight arm arc

Diagram 1-1
Center snap action.

Diagram 1-2
Center snap skidding the ball off left buttocks (the darkened area)
with the right end of the ball slightly up.

COMMON CENTER-TO-QUARTERBACK EXCHANGE PROBLEMS

Miscues are usually the result of some error in technique. The most common is the center's failure to pump the ball straight to the target while attempting to split the wedge of the quarterback's hands. In this case, the center usually tries to lift or swing the ball. This causes the ball to slap the quarterback's top hand and then fall straight toward the ground. If the quarterback is lucky, he might be able to grab the ball with his bottom hand. However, his timing, balance, and control of the ball will probably be thrown off.

If the center fails to skid the ball off his left buttock, and instead places the ball directly on the seam of his pants, the quarterback will end up gripping the ball uncomfortably toward the pointed end. Conversely, if the ball is skidded too far left, the quarterback will grip the ball too close to the other end. Either case can easily lead to a breakdown in timing or a fumble.

Other center-to-quarterback exchange problems that can upset a play are early snaps that catch the quarterback by surprise, too late a snap after the quarterback has already started backwards, or premature pulling away of the quarterback's hands. Any of these errors can lead to a fumble, loss of down, loss of yardage or loss of possession.

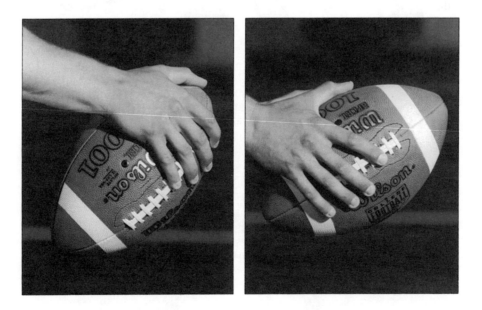

**Ball skidded off pants seam
resulting in poor top grip**   **Ball skidded too far to left
resulting in poor bottom grip**

**Figure 1-2
Poor grips of the ball by the quarterback due to incorrect skidding
of the ball by the center.**

"GOOSING" FOR THE FOOTBALL

For a surprise quarterback sneak, when the quarterback sees the defense is vulnerable to such an attack, the quarterback's "goosing" action to the center is a viable strategy. Two important points must be kept in mind when this impromptu action is used. First, the quarterback must apply "goosing" pressure to the center by lifting both his hands together, in order to keep his hand position unchanged and to give the center a consistent target. Obviously, a change in hand position could result in mishandling the ball on the exchange.

Secondly, the center must be sure to follow through with his usual straight-line pumping delivery to split the "V" of the quarterback's hands. Often the center is caught off guard and changes his delivery, either swinging or lifting the ball. To assure a consistent surprise snap, the center and quarterback should regularly rehearse this situation in practice at times when the center is not expecting the "goose" signal, in order to ensure smooth "goosing" action into their play.

OFFSIDE SNAP

Another surprise snap that should be worked into the center-to-quarterback exchange repertoire is snapping the ball quickly when a defender has jumped offsides. Whether the result of a "long-count," or simply an overly anxious defender, the center and quarterback must be prepared to take advantage of the situation. Just as in the "goose" snap play, the center must be sure to pump the ball straight into the wedge of the quarterback's hands, attempting to split the "V." He must not lift or arc the ball. He must be prepared to not let the element of surprise change his routine delivery.

The center must also be careful that the defender has actually crossed into the neutral zone. A defender may jump forward without actually crossing the neutral zone. In this case, the early snap of the ball could throw off the timing of the offensive play, or even draw an offensive penalty, rather than "catch" the defense offsides.

WET BALL SNAPS

The snapping of a football on wet grass or turf necessitates a definite teaching technique. The proper technique enables the center to place the driest portion of the football in the quarterback's hands. The first step is to have the referee place the ball on the ground so that the laces face directly out toward the sideline, to the center's right. As the center addresses and reaches for the ball, he simultaneously lifts and twists the ball toward himself so the laces are straight up, and he angles the ball on the maximum 45-degree axis allowed. As he lifts and twists the ball to this position, the center attempts to allow as little of the ball as possible to contact the wet ground. In this way, only the portions of the ball's surface darkened in Diagram 1-3 become wet. Neither of these wet spots is detrimental to the center's snapping or the quarterback's reception and grip of the ball.

Diagram 1-3
Portions of the ball that are wet via the wet ball snap technique.

It is also important to occasionally practice the snap of a thoroughly wet ball to enable the center and quarterback to feel comfortable in such a situation. It is important to include a "Bucket Day" (i.e., wetting the ball in a pail of water or with a wet towel) in the practice routine prior to a predicted wet weather game day. This will prepare not only the center and quarterback, but also the backs and receivers, for sure handling of wet balls.

CENTER-TO-QUARTERBACK EXCHANGE PRACTICE AND DRILLS

"Practice makes perfect." Not quite. Incorrect practice can create nightmares. Only "perfect practice makes perfect." Therefore, absolutely every snap from the center should include the complete, correct exchange technique. This is true whether it is a skeleton pass scrimmage, backfield timing practice, or a full-contact scrimmage, as long as a quarterback is receiving a snap from a center. Even though the practice activity may focus mainly on some other aspect of the game, the center-to-quarterback exchange must not be taken for granted. If any incorrect performance of a skill is allowed during any practice, that performance may suddenly appear in a game, often at the most inopportune times.

The center-to-quarterback exchange, therefore, must receive proper attention and coaching in every practice. This need not be overly time-consuming. If the period is well organized and the drill series efficiently run, five to seven minutes will suffice. Pre-practice warm-up is a good time. The following drills develop necessary exchange fundamentals. Some need to be practiced daily, and some only occasionally.

Position of football on ground

Center twist and lift action to 45-degree axis
Figure 1-3
Wet ball snap technique.

Drill #1: Center Pump-Skid Action (Daily)

As soon as the centers arrive at practice, they begin practicing the pumping snap action with a football. The emphasis is on the straight-line pumping action and skidding the ball off the left buttock. The quarterbacks may stand behind the centers and hold only their bottom or downward hand just off the left buttock of the center to see if the ball slaps the hand backwards, signifying proper pumping action that will split the "V" of the quarterback's hands during a normal snap. As a change of pace, the quarterback can place his top hand in normal snap position by itself to see if the ball skids off the heel of the top hand.
A third variation is for the quarterback to just check each pump-skid and comment to the center concerning the proper position of the ball relative to the center's left buttock and/or proper tilt of the ball, right end slightly upward.

Coaching Points: A proper pumping snap will cause the ball to skid off the left buttock. The coach must be sure the ball is not being wrapped around the buttock rather than being skidded. A wrap-around action is the result of lifting or swinging the snap rather than the more reliable pumping action.

Drill #2: Proper Fit (Daily)

The quarterbacks step behind the centers and place their hands in proper snap reception position. Initially, each center brings the ball slowly up to the quarterback's hands and fits it into the wedge until it feels comfortable. Initially, the center can actually drop his head to "look the ball" into the fit. The quarterback adjusts the ball position to the way he wants it delivered. The purpose of this drill is to help develop the kinesthetic feel of the proper positioning of the ball into the quarterback's hands at the end of the snap. After the initial fit, the center takes one or two more half-speed snaps to secure and program this proper fit.

Coaching Points: The quarterback is the coach in this drill. He tells the center how he wants the ball and/or what is wrong with the way the ball is being delivered into his hands.

Drill #3: Closed-Eye Ball Pump (Daily)

The quarterback places his hands in the proper exchange reception position, closes his eyes, and receives pumping snaps from the center. No cadence is used, as all snaps are surprises for the quarterback. Thirty seconds of rapid fire pumping snaps is sufficient. Both center and quarterback must be sure to simulate subsequent movement as they would on any play, the center firing out forward and the quarterback moving away from the center to create a normal game-like situation.

Coaching Points: All of the desired pumping snap aspects are coached. The ball must be wedged between the heels of the quarterback's hands to split the "V." The ball must skid off the left buttock of the center. The laces must arrive where the quarterback wants them, etc.

Drill #4: Cadence Snaps (Daily)

Both the drill and the coaching points are similar to the closed-eye ball pump drill, except that the quarterback keeps his eyes open, and the center snaps off the cadence. One minute is a good time allotment for this drill.

Drill #5: Miscellaneous Cadence and Problem Snaps (Daily)

Drills from this list should be practiced daily. However, the selection and sequence of specific drills should be varied each day. Some are practiced often, and some only occasionally. A checklist should be kept to make sure that all cadences and problems are given an appropriate amount of attention.

- The "goose" snap.
- Snapping on the first sound.
- Audible cadence snapping.
- Long count snapping.
- Quick count snapping.
- Wet ball snaps.
- Late snaps.
- Early snaps.
- Offside snapping: Coach simulates a defensive player.
- Center firing hard away from the quarterback's movement on the snap.
- No snap.

Coaching Points: The practicing of many of these situations is self-explanatory. The coach must be sure, as in the case of the "goose" or late snap, to tell either the quarterback or the center (not both), so that the other player is surprised. Late snaps, for example, refer to a slight delay of the snap by the center, creating a timing problem for the quarterback. The center fires out hard across the line of scrimmage as the quarterback moves out hard in his drop-back in order to help create the most extreme movement problem for the exchange. An occasional "no snap" helps test the quarterback to see if he is releasing the pressure of his hands before the ball comes up.

Drill #6: The Guess-Who Drill

This is a fun-type of drill used as a change of pace. Have a center, with his eyes closed, no-count snap the ball to a quarterback. See if he can guess who the quarterback is. Have a quarterback close his eyes, then place a center in front of him. See if he can guess who the center is. Another variation is to put successive centers in front of the same closed-eye quarterback, or vice versa. Have the quarterback rate the centers who have snapped to him, or have the center rate the quarterbacks who have received his snaps.

Coaching Points: Make sure the individual specifies how he knew who his partner was — something done well, or poorly. This technique can be used to rate quarterbacks or centers.

AUTHOR'S NOTE

In all these drills, the center can fire out into a bag to work on specific types of blocks and to simulate actual game movements. Remember, however, that rapid-fire action is the key to concentrating a lot of exchange practice into a short time period. It is also important that each quarterback work with a different center each day or different centers during the course of one day. In addition, the quarterback must act as a coach in all the drills. The coach can only watch one quarterback-center pair at a time. If the ball hits the top hand, the center must be told. The same is true if the snap is slow, off to one side, etc. Also, some type of forward movement by the center and a pulling away by the quarterback must always occur, except for the center pump-skid action drill and the proper fit drill. These actions are important since a standing-still action by the center and the quarterback practices ungame-like movements, and consequently can lead to the development of bad habits.

BALL-HANDLING SKILLS

SPECIFICITY

A major trend in football coaching is the concept of specificity in practices and practice drills, meaning to develop a psychomotor skill by practicing it in a game-like context. For example, instead of developing hand-eye coordination for a wide receiver in the off-season via handball or racquetball, the receiver is given a set of football catching drills he can practice by himself or with a partner. Thus, he develops specific football hand-eye coordination, not handball or racquetball skills.

On the practice field, this has been taken one step further. Rather than use general football skill drills which may not apply specifically to the requirements of a particular player's position, coaches have instead studied their playbooks, have analyzed what skills are actually performed and then have designed drills that are game-like re-enactments of these skills. Arbitrary drills that do not directly apply to the specific skills of a particular position should be eliminated.

BALL-HANDLING "TRICKS"

Ball-handling is the ability of any back to control the ball, regardless of the situation. It is difficult to create chaotic situations in practice purposely, and it may even be undesirable to do so. One answer is a series of ball-handling drills that can be practiced often, anytime, anywhere, without using valuable team practice time. They also provide excellent pregame warm-up, work off nervousness, pass the time, and still reinforce ball-handling skills. They can be put into a 5-to-7 minute drill routine in a practice period. If encouraged as a fun concept to be played during idle moments, you will be amazed at how much all players who handle the ball will work at them and how adept they will become at controlling the ball.

Since these ball tricks are encouraged on a self-motivated basis, and most players tend to repeat patterns they already do well, the coach must be alert to direct them toward drills for the skills they lack. For example, "Let's see the one-hand juggle....the three ball juggle....try the left hand...."

BALL-HANDLING PRACTICE AND DRILLS (THE BALL "TRICKS")

Drill #1: Iso Grip

This is actually an isometric grip strength exercise. The back simply grips the

19

football in one hand and squeezes it as hard as he can for ten seconds, three repetitions for each hand.

Coaching Points: Be sure the back varies his grip each time: toward the end of the ball, on the fat part, on and off the laces.

Drill #2: Two Man Tug-O-War

Two backs each grip the end of a football, as shown in Diagram 2-1, and steadily try to pull the ball away from each other. It is best to pit right hand against right hand, and vice versa. It can also be done as a one-man isometric exercise. The player grips the ball at each end, holds it at chest level, and pulls against himself. Three sets of ten-second periods are a proper allotment.

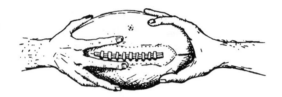

Diagram 2-1
Two man tug-o-war.

Drill #3: Air Dribble

The back holds the ball out in front of his body as show in Diagram 2-2, drops it, catches it as shown, raises it back to its original position, and repeats the drill in rapid-fire succession. Two balls can be used at the same time.

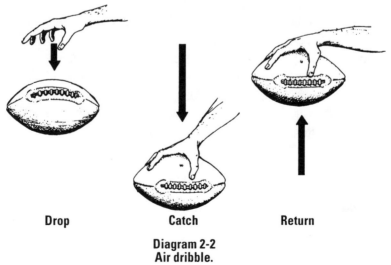

Drop   **Catch**   **Return**

Diagram 2-2
Air dribble.

Drill #4: Ground Dribble

The Ground Dribble Drill is similar to the Air Dribble Drill, except that the back puts one knee down and bounces, or dribbles, the ball off the ground. Two balls can be used here, too.

Drill #5: Forward Hand Roll

The back holds the ball at one end with the palm down (refer to Diagram 2-3). He then rolls the ball over the fingertips to the back of his hand with his palm still facing downward. He then reverses the action to return the ball to its original position. This drill can also be executed with one ball in each hand simultaneously.

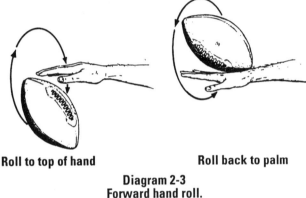

Roll to top of hand   **Roll back to palm**

Diagram 2-3
Forward hand roll.

Drill #6: Forward Finger Flip

This drill is similar to the forward hand roll drill, except that the ball is flipped into the air by the fingers to give it a full back flip, so the ball comes down on the back of the hand. The back of the hand now hits the ball upward to give it a full forward flip so that it returns to its original position (refer to Diagram 2-4).

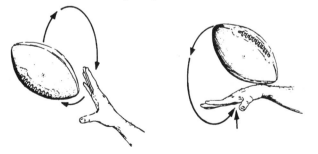

Diagram 2-4
Forward finger flip.

21

Drill #7: Lateral Hand Roll

The back grips the ball at one end with the ball perpendicular to the ground (refer to Diagram 2-5). He then rolls the ball laterally over the back of his hand and grabs it at the opposite end. Then he repeats the action in the opposite direction, returning it to its original position. Again, two balls can be used simultaneously.

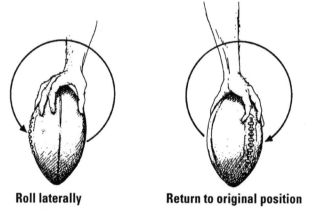

Roll laterally　　　　　　　**Return to original position**

Diagram 2-5
Lateral hand roll.

Drill #8: Hand Circle

This drill is similar to the Air Dribble Drill, except that as the ball is dropped, the player attempts to circle the ball with his hand before he catches it (refer to Diagram 2-6). He should change directions on subsequent repetitions. Two balls add even more of a challenge.

Drill #9: Globe Trotter

The back passes a ball from one hand to the other behind his back, around his head, over his shoulder, through his legs, etc., "Globe Trotter" style, continuously changing directions.

Drill #10: One-Hand Juggle

The player juggles two balls with one hand at a time.

Drill #11: Two-Hand Juggle

The back juggles three balls with two hands in a normal juggling fashion.

Diagram 2-6
Hand circle.

Drill #12: One-Hand Finger Passing

While walking to or from the field, or while standing apart from one another, two backs toss a ball back and forth to one another at a distance of six or seven feet. All catching and tossing is executed by the fingertips. The backs must be sure to switch sides so they work both hands. The coach should stress working the skills that each back performs least proficiently, with extra emphasis on the weaker hand. Added motivation can be created by pitting the backs against each other. Who is the best juggler? Pitting the halfbacks against the quarterbacks or the fullbacks helps stir competition and create a fun and challenging learning environment.

BACKFIELD STANCES AND TAKE-OFFS

Many coaches feel that ball carrying, the skill of running with the football, is simply a natural talent. Either a player has it, or he doesn't. In many instances, such an assertion may be true. Some naturally gifted runners undoubtedly exist. The coach's role, however, is to help each player, however talented, to reach his full potential, and thus enable the team to function at its highest capacity.

Whether your backs are naturally gifted or not, three aspects of running with the football exist that can be developed to each individual's fullest potential: an explosive take-off, acceleration through the open hole, and north-south open-field running. The second two will be discussed in Section II, "Running for Touchdowns."

BACKFIELD STANCES

The quarterback's stance was previously discussed in Chapter 1, so this chapter will concentrate on the other members of the backfield. Since starting different plays from different stances can reveal the play to the defense, most plays should start from a balanced yet explosive stance. Leaning too far forward can tip off a dive play, or sitting too far back in the stance can alert the defense to a pass play. The key is to disguise the variations. For example, a back can ease the pressure off his front hand to facilitate a lateral sweep movement by placing more weight on his heels, and yet still make the stance look as it would for any other type of play.

A back executes an explosive two-point stance, as shown in Figure 3-1, by placing his hands flatly on top of his thighs, arching his back and sticking out his chest, and holding his head up to study the defense, in order to take advantage of the blocking schemes. He concentrates on facing all body parts straight ahead. His feet should be perpendicular to the line of scrimmage, his toes and knees pointed straight ahead, with no lean or twist of his upper torso. Some coaches even prefer a slight inward turning of the toes for a better turf grip with the inner portion of the foot, to insure a more explosive take-off. The back avoids any flat-footedness or hunching over, which would tend to slow down his take-off.

In three-and four-point stances, having the knees pointed straight ahead is even more of a concern. The back may tend to turn the knee of the back leg inward and therefore detract from the desired evenly balanced stance that best facilitates all types of take-offs.

In the three-point stance, the back's weight is evenly distributed on the down hand and two feet. The down hand rests on a bridge formed by the finger

25

Figure 3-1
Two-point stance.

tips. A five-fingered bridge enables more weight on the down hand. A three-fingered bridge formed by only the three middle fingers creates a more balanced distribution of the body weight. Which of these techniques is taught is a matter of the coach's personal preference. It is important, however, that the back doesn't vary the finger-bridge technique, providing a possible defensive key. The down hand bridge is placed just inside the down hand's shoulder.

The player's back should be parallel to the ground, or at a slight downward angle with the butt slightly higher than the shoulders. Remember that it is extremely important that feet and knees are all pointed straight ahead. Inner collapse of the knee off the line, perpendicular to the line of scrimmage, must not occur. Any turning of feet or knees will detract from a balance stance and slow the back's take-off. The heels are slightly raised off the ground.

The foot stagger should never be more than heel to toe. Which foot is forward or back is a coaching preference. Some coaches allow their backs to stagger whichever foot they want. Some specify a left-foot stagger on the left, and right-foot stagger on the right, so that outside feet are always back. Others will always stagger the inside feet. Having backs always stagger the same foot, inside or outside, does have the advantage of consistent handoffs for the quarterback to either side, since the back's steps will be mirrored from either side.

The downback should keep his head up enough to look through the legs of the guard, in order to be aware of any defensive alignment change, but not so high as to be uncomfortable, which would tend to detract from his concentration on his take-off techniques. The back may not be able to see much alignment change, but a sudden defensive movement in which a defensive tackle slides to a head-up position on the guard when he was previously covered by a linebacker may indicate which blocking scheme adjustment is needed. In any case, keeping his head up will help the back be aware of possible blocking adjustments.

The free hand in the three-point stance has an extremely important function. It should be held in a ready position to slide up to the bottom of the stomach to form a handoff pouch (refer to Figure 3-2).

Figure 3-2
Ready position of the free hand in a three-point stance.

In the ready position, the hand is held palm up, facing the back's own face, with the thumb pointing toward the line of scrimmage and downward. The fingers are spread, tense, and hyperextended backward as if they were trying to reach toward the ground. The forearm rests just above the knee. This may seem a bit unorthodox, but the position of the free hand helps to form the handoff pouch. The hand needs only to slide up to the bottom of the stomach. The purpose of such an exaggerated holding of the hand is to ensure the supine (palm up) position of the hand when the handoff pouch is formed, so that the fingers are hyperextended downward with the thumb also facing downward and away from the body. Thus, the fingers won't interfere with the arrival of the football during the handoff. Too many fumbles have resulted when backs have started with their fingers curled, or

27

even in a fist, and failed to open them in time to cleanly receive the handoff. It is important that all the backs utilize this ready position of the free hand on all plays to avoid creating a defensive key.

The four-point stance is usually used by the fullback or upback. It is intended to add an explosive thrust to a forward or slanting take-off by putting more weight forward. This extra thrust is gained at the expense of lateral movement or readiness to pass-block, unless the back sits back on his heels. However, sitting back can be dangerous if it provides a visible key to the defense.

The four-point stance also uses the fingertip bridge. Both hands are placed approximately directly in front of the shoulders, with the fingers about 3 to 6 inches closer to the line of scrimmage. This stance usually has a more downward pitch of the back, with the butt higher than the shoulders, stressing the forward placement of body weight. The heels are raised off the ground a great deal more than in the three-point stance. The feet are evenly spaced with little or no foot stagger, allowing for efficient take-off in either direction.

Although specific guidelines have been given, it is important to note that stance is still an individualized concept. No two players will utilize identical stances. There is no such thing as "the perfect stance." The best stance is one that will enable a back to perform all the required take-offs he must execute in the offense. Sometimes, a coach must deviate to accommodate a player's unique physical characteristics. Of course, this is true of any skill. The purpose of coaching is to help each individual fulfill his true potential. To change a skill that is being done successfully merely for the sake of style, or to "do it by the book," can be a grave coaching error.

EXPLOSIVE TAKE-OFFS VIA THE STEP TECHNIQUE

The step technique for executing an explosive take-off is a sprinter's type of take-off which places all concentration on explosively ripping out the step foot (the foot the back initially steps out with). The only concentration on the other foot, the power foot, is that it is firmly planted.

In the step technique, two goals exist. The back tries to get maximum thrust or power from the planted foot while reaching maximum stepping distance with the step foot. If he concentrates mostly on the pushing off action from the power foot, he will get maximum thrust, but will not achieve maximum stepping distance toward the line of scrimmage with the step foot. In addition, over-emphasis on pushing off the power foot will cause him to rise up and slow his forward movement toward his running landmark. Even a six inch longer step from proper concentration on the step foot could get the back past a linebacker who might otherwise be able to grab an ankle as he breaks across the line of scrimmage.

Concentrating on ripping out the step foot as explosively as possible will automatically cause maximum thrust off the power foot, and yet keep the concentration forward for maximum speed and distance. The natural, lower body-carriage will also create more power as the back approaches the line of scrimmage.

Another important aspect of the step technique for explosive take-off is keeping the elbows in close to the body. If the elbows break away from the body, a natural tendency to raise the upper torso occurs, again costing speed and power. Keeping the elbows in tight to the body enables the back to achieve a low, hard, speedy drive to the line of scrimmage. In addition, whipping the elbow opposite the step foot backwards will actually help the back's step foot and upper torso whip forward more quickly and powerfully.

THE DIVE TAKE-OFF

The dive take-off utilizes the step technique to the utmost in order to create an explosive take-off. All concentration is placed on explosively ripping out the step foot. This would usually be the rear foot, if the feet are staggered. Consistently using the inside foot as the rear foot in a split backfield alignment creates a uniform handoff coordination for the quarterback and running backs for the same play from either side. Some coaches prefer using the inside foot as the step foot whether it is the forward or the rear foot. Using the up foot as the step foot does not produce as explosive a step foot. However, since the up foot is already closer to the dive landmark, little difference in the end result occurs. Thus, whether the inside foot or the rear foot is always used as the step foot becomes a matter of coaching preference.

The explosiveness of the take-off can be enhanced when the rear foot is being used as the step foot if the back anticipates the snap count and shifts his weight to his front, or power foot, just as the snap is about to be called. This enables the back to roll off the power foot as he rips out the step foot. The back must be careful, however, that he is not in motion on this weight shift. He also must be sure to keep his elbows in tight to ensure a low, powerfully gathered attack on the line of scrimmage. Any opening of the elbows will cause a standing up action with a resultant loss of speed and power.

THE OFF-TACKLE TAKE-OFF

The off-tackle take-off, which also utilizes the step technique, is used for such actions as the kick-out block, the off-tackle carry, and the cut block. If the outside foot is the back foot, the step technique is simply executed by ripping out the back foot toward the intended landmark as quickly and explosively as possible. This produces the desired maximum thrust off the front power foot and maximum stepping distance with the rear step foot.

If the inside foot is the rear foot, it should be used as the step foot with an explosive crossover action. Coaches argue the pros and cons of the crossover step for such off-tackle and end run action. Careful film study shows a clear advantage exists in utilizing a crossover step with the rear foot, as compared to using the outside foot for the lead step when it is the up foot. Lead stepping with the outside foot when it is the up foot almost always results in the lead step coming down almost exactly on the same spot where it started. At best, this foot only gains 3 to 4 inches of distance. This is not an explosive lead step. It's a false or wasted step, with no distance gained, but valuable time lost. The crossover step from the rear foot, however, will gain valuable ground as it is ripped out via the step technique. If you measure the distance to the desired landmark covered in the back's first two steps, you will consistently find that the back is closer to the line of scrimmage, therefore "faster off the ball," using the crossover technique.

The crossover step with the inside foot if it is the rear foot helps to ensure the desired inside angle for the kick-out block. It does, however, hinder the desired outside-in course of the cut block. Many coaches will sacrifice the more explosive inside rear foot crossover step for the better outside-in course that the outside foot lead step allows. Others feel that the outside-in angle can still be maintained when utilizing the crossover technique, and therefore get the better, more explosive take-off.

It is important to emphasize again the need for keeping the elbows in close to the body to ensure a low, powerfully gathered stance and prevent loss of speed and power from standing up.

THE END RUN TAKE-OFF

When taking off for the corner, whether to block or carry the ball, the crossover technique provides the best stepping action. This is true no matter which foot is staggered. As previously discussed, lead stepping with the outside foot will do little more than lift and replace the foot on the same spot. In contrast, the cross-over technique will create a significant gain of yardage.

Whipping the outside elbow enhances the crossover technique. Since the crossover is actually a bit unnatural, the concentrated effort to whip back the elbow on the same side as the intended direction of movement helps propel the inside foot across. Again, it's important to keep the elbows in tight. Opening up, with the elbows out, and raising up are natural tendencies in such an outside lateral take-off action, and must be resisted to prevent loss of speed and power.

When aligned in a split backfield set, as shown in Diagram 3-1, a sweeping ballcarrier must make a slight adjustment on his initial crossover step technique so as to help provide a good handoff connection with the quarterback. A direct crossover step makes it difficult for the quarterback to securely execute a handoff, due to the distance the quarterback has to maneuver to reach the deep-ened alignment. Thus, the sweeping split-back ballcarrier must step up slightly toward the line of scrimmage on an approximate 60-degree angle crossover step in order to accommodate the quarterback by providing a good connection point. The ballcarrier must be sure that he steps up with his body aligned so that his handoff pouch is over his initial step foot. After the initial crossover step up toward the line of scrimmage, and the subsequent handoff, the ballcarrier bellies back to get into his normal sweep pattern (refer to Diagram 3-1).

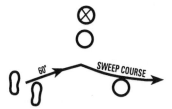

Diagram 3-1
Sixty-degree initial up-into-the-line-of-scrimmage crossover
step for a split-back halfback on a sweep play.

THE COUNTER-STEP TAKE-OFF

The use of the counter step to create a misdirection fake has become increasingly common. After the initial counter-step plant, the usual explosive step technique can be used, with the step foot ripped out in the desired direction. The tight elbow emphasis is again necessary, because as in end-run action, the tendency is to open up the elbows and raise the torso.

The counter step take-off requires some definite coaching points. The counter step should be taken only to an approximate 45-degree angle. Overstep-ping to 90 degrees is unnecessary and actually slows down the back's take-off (refer to Diagram 3-2).

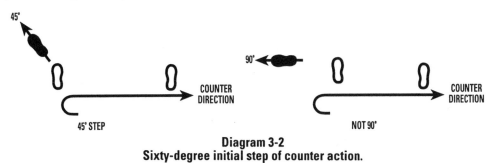

Diagram 3-2
Sixty-degree initial step of counter action.

The 45-degree counter step allows for a good plant of the power foot from which to drive into the step technique with the other foot, because the cleats or turf shoes will get a firm bite.

In addition, the body turn on the counter action need not be more than a 45-degree turn that would place the body weight over the planted counter-step foot. Any more of a body turn only slows down the take-off. Remember that the purpose of the counter step is to influence false flow by the linebacker. Overstepping with the counter foot will properly influence the linebacker, but will also give him time to recover, because by overstepping, the back slows down his own subsequent take-off. Again, the elbow whip action is extremely important for both propelling the change of direction and for keeping the body low.

THE COUNTER-DIVE TAKE-OFF

The counter diveback executes his normal step technique take-off to the line of scrimmage, with one major exception. The diveback's first step rips out in both a lateral and forward direction, with the foot placed down on the ground perpendicular to the line of scrimmage (refer to Diagram 3-3). This step puts the ballcarrier on a path directly into the center-guard gap. Such action gives a slight lateral, counter-type action, while allowing for a quick-hitting, explosive start toward the line of scrimmage.

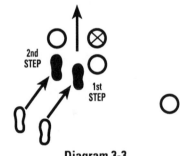

Diagram 3-3
Lateral, ball forward, counter-drive step.

THE QUICK-PITCH/SWING-PASS PATTERN TAKE-OFF

The quick-pitch and swing-pass pattern take-off calls for slightly different footwork by the back (refer to Diagram 3-4). Initially, the back takes a slight 6-inch position step, or set step, with the inside foot. This step actually crosses over slightly to help facilitate the second step, which is toward the sideline. This second step is really a ripping step straight toward the sideline. This action initiates the quick, flat action desired for quick-pitch or swing-pass type plays.

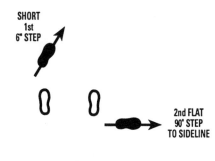

SHORT
1st
6" STEP

2nd FLAT
90° STEP
TO SIDELINE

Diagram 3-4
Quick-pitch/swing-pass pattern take-off.

TAILBACK "I" FORMATION TAKE-OFFS

The action of the tailback must often be altered for different plays. Since both feet are usually kept even, or nearly even, few problems exist in attacking straight ahead or off-tackle. The tailback will, however, often feel the need for a slight drop step to get good footing so he can explode forward on, for example, an isolation play. Some coaches feel that this step should be eliminated, since it is false movement, and instead have the tailback concentrate on a direct step using the step technique. Other coaches feel this is not a problem, since the delay often works well with the running-to-daylight concept of the "I" formation running game. Either technique is correct, so it's more a matter of coaching preference than correctness.

The end run take-off again utilizes the crossover technique. The counter step, however, plays an important role for the tailback, especially when tied to the option game. Since the tailback lines up deeper than a normal fullback or half-back, he must step up initially to maintain the quarterback's usual pitch distance, whatever that may be. Thus, the design of "I" offense plays will often tie together the counter step and the stepping up action to facilitate the tailback's coordination with the fullback (upback) and the quarterback. The only difference from normal counter stepping is a longer step toward the line of scrimmage and a little less than the usual 45-degree angle—more like 30 degrees (refer to Diagram 3-5). Less of a counter step calls for less body lean into the counter action. Instead, a heavy forward motion in the counter-step action occurs, which then translates into the change of direction into the second step. Counter stepping action from the "I" is by no means limited to option plays.

It must be noted that whether using the counter step or not, the tailback does not have to step up on an option play to maintain a halfback or fullback-depth pitch ratio with the quarterback. A tailback could go directly into his pitchback course from his approximate 6-1/2 or 7-yard depth and maintain a deeper ratio with the quarterback. Many "I" formation teams prefer the deepened ratio,

Diagram 3-5
Tailback counter stepping action.

especially when they have a speedy tailback. From the deepened ratio, the tailback may have better cutting angles, especially on "I" isolation and sprint-draw plays.

The tailback's sprint-draw take-off to the exchange point is quite different from any other ballcarrier's (refer to Diagram 3-6). The first step is an open hip lateral step toward the sideline to help create defensive corner flow. This step also helps to delay the draw action long enough for the blocking scheme to develop, as well as to help create a deep handoff point to enable the tailback to make the best cut off the blocking scheme. The second step is a crossover step on an approximate 45-degree angle to the line of scrimmage. The third step is a combination of the rip, or explosion step, and an adjustment step, which attempts to square the ballcarrier to the line of scrimmage, facilitating the possibility of a wide variety of cutting angles for the tailback, and opening his inside hip to the quarterback to allow a proper handoff pouch.

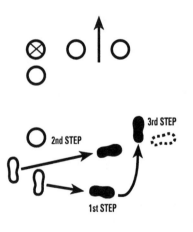

Diagram 3-6
Tailback sprint-draw steps.

34

Proper coaching emphasis must be placed on not gaining too much ground toward the line of scrimmage during the three-step movement to the exchange point. Also, the third step must be squared up to facilitate the handoff. The tailback must not continue out laterally, as this will only make cutting across the grain more difficult, if that is where the daylight is. In addition, the inside hip of the ballcarrier will be closed to the quarterback, necessitating a more difficult reach around the hip to execute the handoff.

It has become increasingly popular for some teams to utilize a sprint-draw tailback take-off technique identical to the tailback isolation take-off. The tailback takes his slight drop step for good footing, from which to explode forward, and executes the same isolation play take-off action. Of course, the design, blocking scheme, and subsequent running action take on the true sprint-draw play design. Thus, a team can run two plays, the sprint draw and the isolation, off the same backfield action.

The limiting factor in the use of the isolation play design for the sprint draw is that the exchange point for the quarterback and the sprint-draw tailback is closer to center area. Therefore, the quarterback cannot threaten the perimeter as well, since he will take more time to attack the corner on his sprint-draw sprint-out action. Since this perimeter sprint-out threat by the quarterback can be so important in the sprint-draw/sprint-draw play-action sprint-out pass series, the effects of a lessened threat of perimeter attack must be weighed against the advantages of the isolation-type take-off.

STANCE AND TAKE-OFF PRACTICE AND DRILLS

Practicing stances and take-offs is usually not set apart in specific drills and practice time, due to the need for compact practice planning and time utilization, except early in the season when the most basic fundamentals are being taught or reviewed. This doesn't mean that stances and take-offs are not practiced during the season. They are practiced every day all through practice. Every drill and every individual, unit, or take-off practice requires the backs to start from a stance and utilize a take-off technique. Each situation offers the coach an opportunity for coaching the stance and take-off.

The following two drills help coach stances and take-offs. The Chute Drill is an excellent early season drill to help develop low, hard-driving take-offs, utilizing the step technique after a proper stance has been checked. The Stance, Take-Off, and Landmark Drill is an excellent early season, as well as in-season drill, that helps to polish exact and precise stances, take-offs, and precise hitting of assigned landmarks. It is excellent in-season because of the continuing need for such execution, coupled with the fact that game preparation for a specific opponent often leads to the neglect of certain fundamentals. The Stance, Take-

Off, and Landmark Drill allows maximum repetition of these important skills in a short time period. The "Landmark" is the point the back aims toward to bring him to the correct exchange point before he cuts off into the blocking scheme.

Drill #1: Chute

The backs, off a quarterback's or coach's cadence, explode from their stances through a normal lineman's chute (refer to Diagram 3-7).
Quarterbacks can be added to add the dimension of handoff practice. The backs must practice firing straight ahead, as well as taking a stance on a 45-degree angle to the chute opening, both left and right, to practice slanting take-offs in each direction.

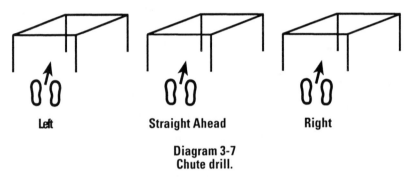

Left   Straight Ahead   Right

**Diagram 3-7
Chute drill.**

Coaching Points: When working on the angled take-off, the back's stance should face the opposite back post of the chute. The coach must be sure to check all points of stance and take-off (step technique). Crossover stepping for off-tackle and end-run action is difficult to practice through a chute, due to the higher carriage of the body in such action.

Drill #2: Stance, Take-Off, and Landmark

The backs take their proper alignment relative to a line spacing tape (refer to Diagram 3-8), and run the play assignment call given by the coach. Two backs can usually go at the same time to execute, for example, two dives, thus allowing more repetitions. A quarterback or the coach gives the proper cadence call.

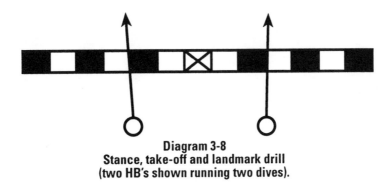

Diagram 3-8
Stance, take-off and landmark drill
(two HB's shown running two dives).

Coaching Points: The coach must be sure to check all points of stance, take-off, and landmarks. He must also be sure to carefully plan that all actions are covered or at least the ones he wants covered in the drill (e.g., quick-pitch, sweep, counter dive, etc.).

CHAPTER 4

QUARTERBACK-BALLCARRIER EXCHANGE TECHNIQUES

As mentioned in Chapter 1, unless the quarterback keeps the ball himself, some type of ball exchange must occur between the quarterback and another back or receiver. The exchange might be in the form of a handoff, a toss, a quick pitch, an option pitch or a pass. Whatever technique is used, the ball exchange creates one of the most critical situations the offense faces. A poor handoff or pitch may result in a fumble and loss of ball possession, or even a defensive score. An offensive scoring opportunity can quickly turn into a demoralizing miscue.

Because the quarterback-ballcarrier exchange is such a critical skill, it must receive careful coaching and practice, and must become as fail-safe as the center-to-quarterback exchange. All chance of error must be absolutely minimized. The focus, therefore, must be on the precise execution of the exchange skills. The smallest variation cannot be tolerated, because being "slightly off" can result in a disastrous fumble.

QUARTERBACK MOVEMENT TO THE EXCHANGE POINT

Upon receiving the snap, the quarterback must immediately bring the ball to his "third hand"—his stomach. This helps secure and protect the ball from any immediate defensive pressure, whether the quarterback can see it or not. The quarterback's hands are positioned so that his fingers run parallel to the long axis of the ball. The fingers are comfortably spread to securely envelop the ball. It is extremely important that the quarterback keep his shoulders at the same elevation from the ground throughout the entire movement from his stance to the handoff or pitch, in order to create an absolutely consistent mesh with the ballcarrier, or a consistent delivery of the pitch or toss. If the quarterback, especially a tall one, raises up as he pivots to mesh for a dive handoff, for example, he will have to handoff with a downward movement. Since the diveback is moving in a low, powerfully gathered stance, the quarterback's handoff might easily hit the upper arm of the diveback as the quarterback attempts to put the ball into the diveback's pouch. Hitting the pouch off-center can easily cause a handling miscue, or worse, a fumble.

The reverse pivot toss is another prime example of the need for keeping the quarterback's shoulders at the same elevation throughout his movement to the exchange point. Since the flight of the pitch is directly related to the follow-through action of the quarterback's arms and hands, a raising of the shoulders will normally cause a higher release, and thus a higher toss. Consistent ball exchanging demands that the quarterback maintain his shoulders at the same level from the snap reception through the exchange. The total set of quarterback movements to the exchange point will be discussed separately under each specific type of exchange.

THE QUARTERBACK HANDOFF TECHNIQUE

The quarterback secures the ball against his stomach, "the third hand," until the moment of delivery into the ballcarrier's pouch. The quarterback must immediately find the spot in the ballcarrier's stomach that is dead center of the pouch. He must concentrate so intently on this spot throughout the handoff action that he actually attempts to see the ball make contact with the precise spot. This concentration is similar to that of a baseball player trying to actually see the bat contact the ball.

Anything less than hitting the exact spot is incorrect. Even slight deviations can be disastrous. A handoff not delivered to the center of the pouch can hit the hip bone or the bottom of the shoulder pads and cause a fumble. At best, the ballcarrier still might not get a firm grip on the ball.

The best handoff is a firm two-handed handoff, enabling security and control of the ball all the way from the snap into the ballcarrier's pouch, always in a level position or parallel to the ground. A one-handed handoff often results in the ball's being placed into the ballcarrier's pouch at varying spots, with varying tilts, resulting in a less secure exchange.

The handoff actually is made in two stages. First, the quarterback firmly places the ball on the spot, with both hands on the ball, and with the back of the inside hand actually placed directly on the spot. A firm placement is what helps signal the ballcarrier to fold his arms over the ball. Anything less than a firm placement allows unwanted movement of the ball within the ballcarrier's pouch.

The second stage of the handoff is to push the ball up against the spot with the outside hand, as the inside hand slides out from behind the ball. The inside hand remains close to the ball, so it can be brought back to the quarterback's body simultaneously with the outside hand, creating a good quarterback hand fake action. This type of faking movement by the quarterback depends on the action of the play's design.

Whatever type of play action is employed in the handoff, the quarterback must be sure that his stepping and subsequent foot and leg positioning do not interfere with the ballcarrier's running action. The quarterback might have to take an exaggerated adjustment step, or take a drag or hesitation step, in which the step leg is limply delayed to allow the ballcarrier to pass by before the step foot is placed on the ground. The quarterback must realize that all concentration and effort are placed first on a perfect handoff. All faking action comes after the execution of the perfect handoff.

**Anything less than the quarterback hitting the
exact spot on a handoff is incorrect.**

Another important idea to keep in mind is that all handoffs should be made as deeply behind the line as possible. This is especially true on dive plays, due to the desire for an explosive hit on the line of scrimmage by the ballcarrier. The deeper handoff assures both maximum momentum buildup and the best cutting angles for the ballcarrier in his efforts to run to daylight.

BALLCARRIER'S RECEPTION OF HANDOFF

The ballcarrier's handoff pouch is created by making a lateral "V" position of the arms, as shown in Figure 4-1, so the ball can be naturally placed on the spot. The bottom, or outside hand is lifted to the belt buckle area, palm up, with the pinkie close to the belt buckle, and the fingers spread almost taut and hyperextended downward toward the ground, so they do not interfere with the handoff.

Figure 4-1
Ballcarrier pouch.

The top, or inside arm, is whipped upward to raise the inside elbow as high as possible so that it does not interfere with the handoff. Turning the thumb of the top hand inward and downward will help raise the inside elbow properly.

It is extremely important for the ballcarrier to not look at the quarterback's handoff action, nor attempt to watch the ball. The backs must understand that the handoff action is the quarterback's responsibility. The ballcarrier's job is to fix his eyes straight ahead to study the blocking scheme, so he can break to daylight after receiving the ball.

Another important concept for both the ballcarrier and the quarterback is that of the explosive take-off toward the prescribed landmark designated by the design of the play. The landmark is the ballcarrier's initial aiming point (e.g., outside hip of the guard on a dive play), which provides a constant mesh point for the quarterback. The ballcarrier must never vary or veer from this course until after the handoff has been completed. This will ensure a consistent mesh point for the handoff every single time a specific play is run. All of the ballcarrier's breaking to daylight is done, therefore, after completion of the handoff. This may make breaking to daylight more difficult, but a good quarterback-ballcarrier exchange is critical to the success of any running play.

The back must be careful not to hunch or bend over as he forms his pouch to receive the handoff. Such action causes the upper arm and elbow to become an obstacle to the quarterback's handoff action.

The back's running action and his formation of the pouch must exist as two separate entities. He must create a steady pouch target for the quarterback that does not bounce or jiggle with this running action. The actual reception is made by a folding or closing of the arms over the ball, not harshly, but attempting to envelop the ball to secure it in the armpit of the bottom arm. Once secured, a one-armed carry is essential. A running back should never attempt to carry the ball in two hands in front of the body, because if it's not tucked under an armpit, the ball is too vulnerable. A proper two-handed carry is actually a one-handed carry with the ball securely tucked under one armpit, with the opposite arm and hand placed over the top of the ball to shield and protect it.

QUARTERBACK REVERSE PIVOT ACTION

The reverse pivot is commonly used in many types of offenses. No one single technique exists, however, because the quarterback's steps are determined by the handoff point of each play's design. Basically, however, the reverse pivot is a two-step action, as shown in Diagram 4-1. The first step, or drop step, is made with one foot toward the side of the play's action. Its depth into the backfield and width toward the sideline are determined by the handoff point of the play.

For example, an isolation handoff to an "I" set tailback requires a deep drop step with little, if any, lateral movement from center. This action enables the quarterback to deliver the ball deeply, as desired, and yet keeps the quarterback out of the tailback's tight running path.

On the other hand, a reverse pivot hand off to the fullback for an off-tackle run requires a drop step that is wider to one side, and therefore less deep than the "I" isolation drop, as shown in Diagram 4-2.

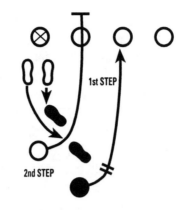

Diagram 4-1
QB reverse pivot steps for "I" isolation play.

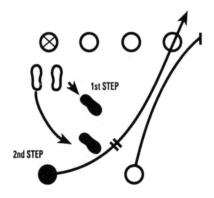

Diagram 4-2
QB reverse pivot steps for pro-set off-tackle run.

In a sweep play to a split-back halfback, as shown in Diagram 4-3, the reverse action pivot also requires a deep initial drop step to enable the quarterback to get to the deep handoff point and still get quickly around in front of the halfback's pouch. The initial deep drop step is followed by either a short adjustment step, or a possible drag/hesitation step, so as not to interfere with the ballcarrier's sweep path. This drag/hesitation step, however, is usually only necessary with a taller, long-legged quarterback. In all these actions, therefore, the initial drop step foot is the pivot foot.

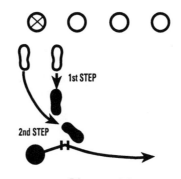

Diagram 4-3
QB reverse pivot steps for split-back sweep run.

A different, special reverse pivot action is necessary to accommodate a tight slicing off-side back to the on-side in, for example, an isolation play, as shown in Diagram 4-4. This technique is designed to get the quarterback out of the ballcarrier's tight path. This "matador" reverse pivot is executed by initially drop-stepping with the off-side foot and pivoting off it. The drop step is not a deep step, similar to the previous isolation-type drop step, since the quarterback must, again, stay out of the ballcarrier's path.

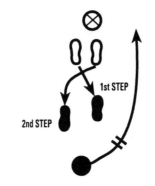

Diagram 4-4
QB "matador" reverse pivot steps for tight run path
to on-side by off-side back.

It is important to remember that no two quarterbacks will take identical step patterns to the exchange point, whether reverse pivot or not. For example, a 6'5" quarterback will naturally step differently than a 5'10" quarterback. The coach must help each individual quarterback to develop the step patterns that will best enable him to effectively accomplish the quarterback-ballcarrier exchange.

QUARTERBACK'S SPRINT-DRAW ACTION

The quarterback's movement to a sprint-draw handoff point takes on its own distinct coaching points. Actually, it's a relatively easy skill. The emphasis in the quarterback's stepping must be to get the ball to the sprint-draw back as deeply as possible, to best facilitate his breaking to daylight off the blocking scheme. The quarterback takes a lead step, crossover step, and an adjustment step. The lead step is a front-out step approximately 150 degrees off the line of scrimmage, as shown in Diagram 4-5.

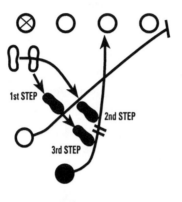

Diagram 4-5
QB sprint-draw steps.

Some coaches feel the quarterback should "look off" the linebackers on the first step. Others prefer to have their quarterbacks immediately look for the handoff spot to the ballcarrier's pouch.

The second step is a crossover step continuing on the 150-degree path of the lead step. It is most important, however, that the quarterback begin adjusting to the mesh point with the ballcarrier.

The third step simply carries out this adjustment, to facilitate a perfect positioning for the handoff. Some coaches have their quarterbacks execute an exaggerated two-handed handoff in which the quarterback is well in front of the ballcarrier, at the expense of a good play-action fake. Others instruct their quarterbacks to execute a one-handed handoff in which the quarterback's and ballcarrier's shoulders are almost parallel, to create a better play-action pass fake. This one-handed handoff, however, is not as secure as a two-handed handoff.

QUARTERBACK'S COUNTER DIVE ACTION

For the counter dive handoff, the quarterback utilizes a four-step counter action, as shown in Diagram 4-6. The initial movement to the dive fake, which is simply a reverse pivot counter fake action, concentrates on the setup of the actual reverse pivot action. The key coaching point is that the emphasis is on delivery of the ball to the counter diveback, not on the initial counter fake.

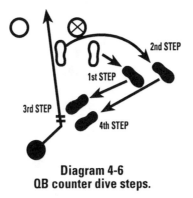

Diagram 4-6
QB counter dive steps.

The quarterback's first step is slightly deeper than a normal dive action step. The second step is a slight crossover step to help set up the reverse step back to the diveback. The third step is the key step. In this, the quarterback steps back to the counter diveback as deeply as possible to execute as deep a handoff as he can. The fourth step is simply a sliding type step as a sort of adjustment step to help the quarterback keep his balance as he finishes executing the handoff.

Again, the emphasis is on the deep third step to the diveback to execute the deep handoff. On the initial step, the quarterback waves the ball in the direction of the dive fake. However, an overfake of the ball will only detract from the important third deep step back to the diveback.

THE QUARTERBACK AND BALLCARRIER'S TECHNIQUES ON DRAW ACTIONS

The quarterback's draw action can vary greatly, depending on the type of drop back setup used by the quarterback. It is important that the draw action develops directly from whatever drop back action is used: back pedal, crossover, or a combination of the two. Whatever technique is used, three important concepts need to be coached. First, the quarterback must "look off" the linebackers during at least the first drop step, by staring out straight ahead. Second, no matter what drop back technique is used, the quarterback must fully open his hip to the draw-back by taking a deep open step 180 degrees from the line of scrimmage, so that the quarterback has a good base from which to execute the handoff. Third, the quarterback must keep in mind that his drop back pass action will cause him to carry his body higher than he would on any other handoff action. Thus, he must take this into account, so he can be sure to get the ball into the pouch of the drawback, underneath the drawback's top arm. Thus, the quarterback must be sure to have the ball low enough prior to delivery so that no interference will occur.

Diagram 4-7 shows the 180-degree opening step of the quarterback off a crossover drop back action on the third step. Whatever step is used as the open step, it must be an adjustment type of step in which the distance is determined by the distance to the handoff point.

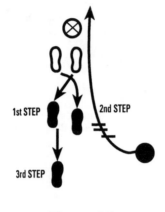

Diagram 4-7
QB draw steps.

The ballcarrier has two major concerns. First, he must realize that the critical situation is the quarterback's higher-than-usual carriage of his body on his drop back action, and, thus, the more difficult handoff mesh. The back must, therefore, be sure to whip the elbow of the top arm up a little more quickly than usual, and be sure that the elbow is exaggeratedly high to help facilitate the handoff mesh.

Second, if the ballcarrier is faking pass protection toward the end of the line of scrimmage, he must do so with the upper torso of his body only. He must keep his inside hip square to the line of scrimmage so that the quarterback has the pouch open to him once the ballcarrier whips up his inside elbow. In this fashion, the quarterback will not have to reach around the ballcarrier's hip to hand the ball off (refer to Figure 4-2).

Hip open to line of scrimmage   **Elbow whipped up to form pouch**

Figure 4-2
Drawback setup faking end rush pass-pro block.

THE QUARTERBACK'S TOSS/QUICK-PITCH

The toss or quick-pitch can come off either a direct front out action (refer to Figure 4-3) or a reverse pivot action (refer to Figure 4-4). Whichever action is used, it is important that the quarterback maintains a level shoulder position to ensure a consistent delivery and follow-through on the toss or quick pitch. All concentration is on a follow-through delivery. The quarterback executes a straight-arm toss or quick-pitch and sights the ball to the delivery point by peering over the fingertips. The palms of his hands should be "taking a picture" of the exact spot that the ball should be delivered to. This spot is a yard-and-a-half in front of the ballcarrier, belt high.

A high or low pitch is usually the result of a follow-through aimed high or low. If the hands are "taking a picture" of the wrong spot, the ball is likely to go there.

The quarterback must also be sure to not lower the ball from his stomach area after receiving the center snap, before he delivers the toss or quick-pitch. Such a "hitch" in the delivery will usually cause the quarterback to overcompensate for the lowering of the ball by releasing the ball higher than desired, with a resultant high trajectory of the toss or quick-pitch.

Figure 4-3
Front out toss/quick-pitch.

Figure 4-4
Reverse pivot toss/quick-pitch.

The difference between executions of the quick-pitch and the toss is that the quick-pitch must quickly get the ball to the ballcarrier who is already well outside of the quarterback. This ball delivery requires a lower trajectory in the flight of the ball due to the ball's greater speed. The follow-through is therefore more pronounced in the quick-pitch.

The toss, on the other hand, need not be as rushed, since the ball can easily be "tossed" to a point that leads the ballcarrier, so it "hangs" a bit, and he catches up to it on his run path. A soft, end-over-end tumble produces the easiest toss for the ballcarrier to receive.

THE QUARTERBACK OPTION-PITCH

A soft, tumbling, end-over-end pitch is the easiest option-type pitch to receive. Therefore, it's the best one for the quarterback to use. A key factor in the success of the option-pitch is the quarterback's prepitch carrying position. He must be sure to carry the ball directly in front of his sternum to assure a proper arcing flight of the ball from the quarterback to the pitchback. A properly executed pitch should be directed to arc to a point approximately a yard-and-a-half in front of the pitchback at belt level. A pitch which originates from the sternum enables the biomechanically correct wrist and hand movement to properly execute the option-pitch. If the ball is held in a low carry, around belt level, the wrist is naturally hindered in its ability to deliver the desired arcing, soft tumbling, end-over-end pitch that will drop at belt-level for the pitchback. Instead, the biomechanical limitations of the wrist and hand will cause the pitch from a low carry position to have a low trajectory in flight, and will likely drop to too low a level for the pitchback, possibly knee level, or worse. Some quarterbacks will actually "sling" the ball from too low a carry position, resulting in a hard pitch that explodes into the pitchback's face.

To produce the soft, tumbling, end-over-end pitch, the quarterback extends his arm and hand out toward the desired pitch point and rotates the wrist so that the thumb pronates downward, allowing the arm, wrist, and hand to produce a combined pushing and flipping of the ball. The trajectory of the ball should look something like that shown in Diagram 4-8.

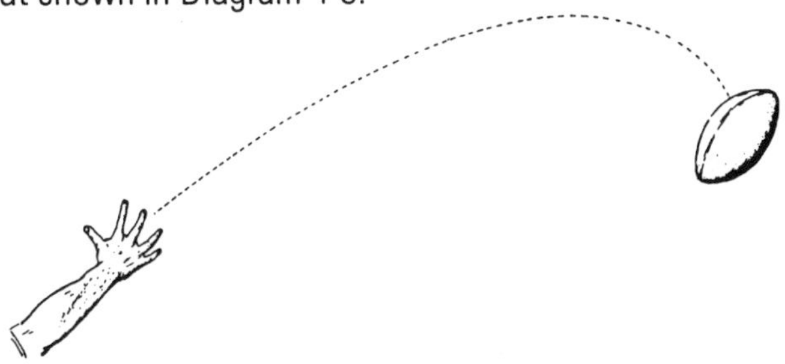

Diagram 4-8
Proper trajectory of the option-pitch.

This trajectory, therefore, takes off sharply and quickly. However, it reaches its zenith approximately two-thirds of the way to the pitchback and falls more softly to the desired pitch point.

Follow-through is also a key to a successful pitch. Proper follow-through is accomplished by having the quarterback "take a picture" with the palm of his pitch hand of the spot where he wants the pitch to go. Concentration on this technique will also aid the rotation of the wrist to pronate the thumb and hand. Figure 4-5 shows the proper sequence of an option-pitch delivery by the quarterback.

BALLCARRIER'S RECEIVING OF THE TOSS, QUICK-PITCH OR OPTION-PITCH

The techniques used to receive either type of pitch or toss are basically the same. The only real difference comes in positioning the hands to receive the ball. Since, however, the arrival of the ball can vary greatly on each of the pitch or toss techniques, one overall technique should be developed for reception of all pitches and tosses.

Concentration by the pitchback is the key to successfully receiving a pitch. He must immediately focus his eyes on the ball in the quarterback's hands upon his first take-off step. He must concentrate on the ball as it is carried by the quarterback, as it leaves the quarterback's hand, as it progresses in flight, and as it reaches his hands. Concentration must be so intense that the pitchback sees the ball make contact with his hands.

The pitchback forms a "basket" with his hands for the ball to fall into (refer to Figure 4-6). The inside hand forms the bottom of the basket, thumb curled downward to prevent interference with the pitch, while the outside hand faces the ball to act as a "backstop" to prevent the pitch from going past. The fingers are open and spread as they are in a normal handoff. Again, the pitchback must be sure to look the ball into his hands. He *must not* attempt to read the blocking scheme until the ball is secured. A major problem, resulting in pitch fumbles, is that the pitchback will take his eyes off the ball a split-second before the reception in an eagerness to read the blocking scheme and will, as a result, end up bobbling or fumbling the ball.

Figure 4-5
Quarterback option-pitch action.

Figure 4-6
Ballcarrier basket-type positioning of the hands to receive a pitch or a toss.

THE REVERSE HANDOFF

The reverse handoff poses the problem of both backs running toward one another at top speed, making the exchange difficult. The back handing the ball off executes all of the proper handoff techniques, i.e., looking the ball into the pouch and placing it on the spot, with one exception—a one-handed handoff technique is used.

The back receiving the reverse handoff, however, must utilize an entirely different technique for forming a pouch, in order to handle the high-speed, single-hand delivery, as shown in Figure 4-7. Instead of a normal "V" shaped pouch, in which there is too much possibility of interference by the top arm, a basket-like pouch is formed with both hands at the bottom of the stomach. As usual, the fingers are spread and taut, ready to trap the ball into the stomach once it has been placed on the spot.

Figure 4-7
Reverse handoff pouch.

QUARTERBACK-BALLCARRIER EXCHANGE PRACTICE AND DRILLS

A coach has a tremendous opportunity to coach the quarterback-ballcarrier exchanges all throughout practice. Since so many of all practice drills start with some type of ball exchange, each situation presents the coach with a distinct coaching opportunity. For this reason, isolated quarterback-ballcarrier drills are often limited to early preseason fundamental work, brush-up timing work or more difficult exchanges, such as the quick-pitch and the option-pitch. Thus, only one option-pitch drill will be presented in this chapter. The rest will be discussed in Chapter 8—"The Backfield Option Game."

Drill #1: Handoff Pouch and Reception

The handoff pouch and reception drill is an excellent preseason drill to utilize when teaching or refining basic fundamentals. It's an odd-looking drill, but is very useful in producing a maximum number of repetitions. In this drill, a group of backs simply jog around aimlessly in an area 15 to 20 yards square. They practice forming a perfect handoff pouch and then practice folding over a pretended handoff action.

Coaching Points: The coach wants to make sure that the handoff pouch is perfect—inside elbow up, fingers spread, almost taut, and hyperextended backwards, etc. The upper-body carry should be disengaged from the lower body's run action for both the handoff pouch and the action of folding over the ball. The coach must be sure to check that the backs practice both left-and right-handed pouches. In addition, the backs must smoothly fold over the ball without any jerking or clamping action. The aimless direction of the drill enables the coach to check the backs' actions from many angles.

Drill #2: Handoff Pouch and Reception Circle

The handoff pouch and reception circle drill takes on all the characteristics of the previous drill, except that the backs are given a set circular course, and the coach is specifically checking frontal pouch and reception action of one back at a time (refer to Diagram 4-9).

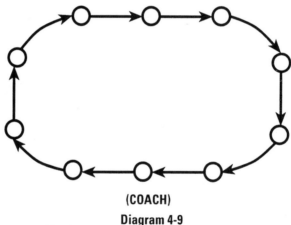

(COACH)
Diagram 4-9
Handoff pouch and reception circle drill.

Drill #3: Timing

The timing drill is perhaps the best drill overall for coaching the quarterback-ballcarrier exchanges. A center may be used to practice the snap exchange as well. Two tapes or hoses are laid on the ground parallel to one another (refer to Diagram 4-10). This layout enables the coach to watch and coach two sets of backfields at the same time. The coach calls out the desired play action and two sets of backs simultaneously execute the appropriate ball exchange techniques.

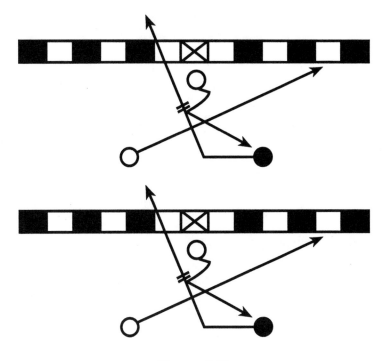

Diagram 4-10
Timing drill
(crossbuck-type action used as an example).

Coaching Points: A quarterback calls out the signals for both sets of backs. The drill is actually a multipurpose drill for such skills as stance, alignment, take-off, landmark, center-quarterback exchange, quarterback-ballcarrier exchange and timing, as well as practice of specific play executions. The coach must be sure to practice specific quarterback-ballcarrier exchanges in desired time ratios, since a dive handoff may not need the amount of practice a quick-pitch exchange needs.

Drill #4: Breakdown

The breakdown drill is simply isolation of a specific aspect of the timing drill to achieve rapid-fire action and maximum repetitions of the more difficult exchanges, such as the quick-pitch, the sprint-draw, or a reverse counter-type action. For example, Diagram 4-11 shows a breakdown drill practicing the rapid-fire quick-pitch action to a line of halfbacks.

Coaching Points: The use of a center for a game-like snap is extremely important to create a game-like situation for the entire action. The coach should be sure to practice to both sides equally, or even practice more to the quarterback's weaker side.

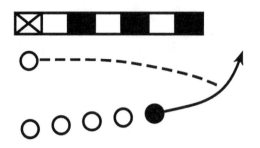

Diagram 4-11
Breakdown Drill
(quick-pitch action used as an example).

Drill #5: Option-Pitching on the Knee

This drill concentrates on the pure hand and arm action of the option-pitch by disengaging the rest of the body. As shown in Figure 4-8, two quarterbacks each kneel on the inside knee and face one another at the desired pitch ratio (i.e., 3-1/2 yards by 3-1/2 yards, or 4 yards by 4 yards, etc.) on the desired 45-degree pitch angle. They simply practice execution of a proper option-pitch—a soft, tumbling, end-over-end pitch.

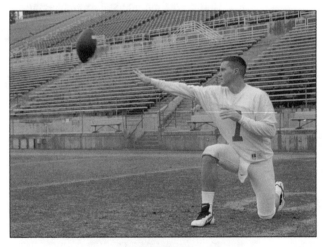

Figure 4-8
Option pitching on the knee drill.

Coaching Points: The quarterbacks could stand. However, the kneeling does help separate the upper torso action from the leg action, since this will often be the action on an option-pitch. Switch their 45-degree angle relationship halfway through the drill period, so they can practice pitching with the opposite hands. The coach might want, once again, to spend extra time on the quarterback's weaker side.

CHAPTER 5

TOTAL BALL SECURITY

Ball security refers to the offense's ability to reliably handle the football and maintain control and possession on all of its play executions. Many of the aspects of ball security have entire chapters devoted to them such as center-quarterback exchanges, quarterback-ballcarrier exchanges, and backfield pass receiving. This chapter will focus on actual ballcarrying security skills, so the ballcarrier does not carry the ball "like a loaf of bread," have the ball "pop out" in a hard collision, or fumble the ball while reaching out to gain an "extra yard."

PROPER CARRYING OF THE FOOTBALL

In a secure carry of the football, the ballcarrier envelops the ball with his hand, fingers, arm, and armpit. He actually tries to cover as much of the ball as possible, leaving as little as possible of the ball's surface exposed. The greater the amount of ball surface exposed, the greater the chance of a fumble. Figure 5-1 shows the proper techniques for carrying the ball securely.

Figure 5-1
Secure carry of the football.

The tip of the football is covered by the spread fingers, as the fingers attempt to squeeze the ball into the armpit in a vise-like locking grip. The elbow plays a key role (refer to Figure 5-2).

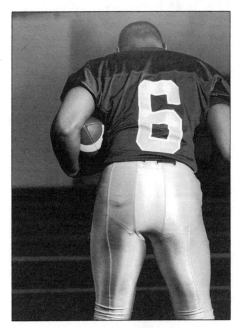 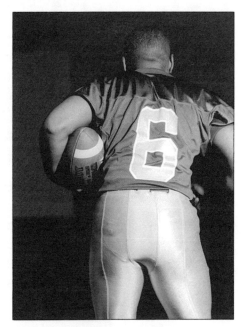

**Proper wrapping around
action of elbow**

**Improper positioning of
elbow out away from the body**

**Figure 5-2
Proper and improper elbow action while carrying the football.**

It must be wrapped around and under the ball, so that all parts of the ball are enveloped within the hand, forearm, and armpit. If the elbow is not wrapped around and under, but is allowed to swing away from the body, the bottom of the ball will be exposed, and a blow to the top of the body will be able to jar it loose. This can easily be demonstrated in practice.

The proper vise-like lock of the ball up into the armpit should secure the ball so tightly that no visible space exists between the top of the ball and the armpit. A good coaching adage is that the coach should "not see air."

THE TWO-ARMED CARRY

Actually, a ballcarrier should *never* carry the ball in two arms. Inevitably, using two arms takes the ball from under his armpit, which is absolutely the most secure place to carry it. A two-handed carry in front of the ballcarrier will often result in the ball "popping out" upon violent impact, or being ripped out by a defender grabbing one arm and pulling it away from the other.

The only proper carry using both hands is actually a normal one-handed carry with the other hand and arm placed over the vise-locked ball to provide extra protection (refer to Figure 5-3). Essentially, the free hand helps to cover more of the ball's surface, while the extra arm helps absorb most of the blow from contact. Whenever a ballcarrier realizes that he is going to have to lower his shoulder to attempt to blast over a defender, he should bring the free hand and arm over to help protect the ball.

Figure 5-3
Two-hand carry of the football.

CHANGING THE BALL FROM ONE HAND TO THE OTHER

Changing the ball from one hand to the other is generally not advisable, especially when the back is close to defensive traffic. During such an exchange, the ball is extremely vulnerable to being knocked loose, or even just dropped. The question then arises, is switching the ball to the other hand ever worth the risk of a fumble? Whatever the answer, the backs must be coached to never attempt to transfer the ball when surrounded by defenders. For example, on a dive play, as the ballcarrier accelerates through a hole, he is in the midst of heavy traffic, and any jarring contact, even with one of his own teammates, could easily jar the ball loose.

At such time as the well-coached ballcarrier deems that switching sides with the ball would protect the ball better, he should execute an exchange technique similar to a normal handoff action, except that the ball is already in the "bottom" hand and arm. The exchange is then executed by taking the free hand and reaching over toward the armpit where the ball is locked, almost as if to form the top arm and hand position of a normal handoff pouch. The free hand reaches over and grips the end of the football under the armpit, then "drags" the ball across, close to the body, and into the opposite armpit, where it is again clamped in a vise-like grip. The hand from the side where the ball was carried remains underneath the ball to help guide it across and into the new armpit. Thus, the hand formerly carrying the ball helps to provide security for the changing action. Next, the ballcarrier must be sure to execute a proper one-armed carry of the ball under the new armpit.

PROBLEM AREAS FOR BALL SECURITY

Specific situations exist that lead to insecure ballcarrying. These situations must be coached and emphasized in practice so improper ballcarrying techniques can be eliminated.

In the dive jump technique, for example, which is discussed in Chapter 7, extending the ball out away from the body to reach for extra yardage is extremely dangerous. Any action in which the ball is removed from the security of the armpit vise exposes a tremendous amount of the ball's surface and renders it very vulnerable to fumbling.

Only under a few extreme situations should reaching out with the football be attempted. They are almost always desperation situations—a last-ditch effort for a touchdown on fourth down, a desperate attempt to get first-down yardage on a critical drive, etc.

Another common ball security error is allowing the ball to open up away from the body on a hard cutting action by the ballcarrier. Again, any action that moves the ball away from the vise-like grip between hand and armpit leads to a greater chance of fumble. This same problem often happens when a ballcarrier attempts to drag or carry a defender and stretches out to get extra yardage.

Two other critical situations that often create poor ball security are when a ballcarrier is rolling and when a ballcarrier is making an extra effort in general. Rolling, as a result of falling or contacting a defender, often results in a loosened carry of the football. The same is true when a ballcarrier is making a second, third, or even fourth effort to struggle forward for extra yardage. The back must be prepared to not let his extra effort lead to a breakdown in concentration on ball security.

BALL SECURITY PRACTICE AND DRILLS

Many opportunities exist for ball security practice in the context of practicing other facets of backfield play. In every drill, the ballcarrier should practice carrying the ball properly. He should rehearse covering the ball with his free hand with every contact in scrimmage. He must keep the ball gripped in an armpit vise every time he dives over a pile of players. The coach should simulate game-like conditions for every facet of backfield practice.

Drill #1: Ball Iso

In the ball iso drill, the backs simply execute a proper one-hand carry of the football and squeeze the ball into their armpits as hard as possible for a ten-second count in an isometric-type exercise. This helps develop the strength needed for the vise-like grip. Be sure to work on both sides equally, or more on the weaker side.

Coaching Points: The backs must attempt to squeeze the ball so hard that they attempt to "squeeze the air out of the ball."

Drill #2: Arm Wrestle

The arm wrestle drill pairs up two backs. One back executes a proper one-arm carry of the ball. The other back wrestles, grabs, rips, punches at the ball, arm, and hand of the ballcarrier in an attempt to separate the ball from the ballcarrier. This action continues for thirty seconds. The ball is switched, using the proper ball transfer technique, and the drill is repeated on the other side.

Coaching Points: Again, extra time can be allotted to the weaker side.

Drill #3: Ball Change

In the ball change drill, the ballcarrier again teams up with another back. He executes his proper ball changing technique from arm to arm while the other back executes the arm wrestle drill, except with emphasis on slapping, punching, and grabbing, rather than actually latching on and wrestling. The ballcarrier must perform a set number of repetitions of the ball change in an allotted time period.

Coaching Points: The arm wrestle drill and the ball change drill can be combined into one drill. The ballcarrier executes a proper one-armed carry while the other back does the arm wrestle drill. Then both backs perform their roles in the ball change drill. This sequence may again be repeated a set number of times in a time period.

Drill #4: Two-Hand Carry

The two-hand carry drill is executed along with a rapid-fire forearm shiver drill. The ballcarrier executes a one-armed carry. Another back sets up slightly to the ballcarrier's right front at an approximate distance of two yards. The coach stands behind the ballcarrier and signals the other back when to unload a blow into the ballcarrier. As the blow is unloaded, the ballcarrier must properly cover the ball with his free hand and arm to execute a proper two-handed carry and absorb the blow. During the delivery of the blow, the other back may add punches, slaps, rips, etc., to try to knock the ball loose. After four or five blows, the ballcarrier switches the ball to his other side as the other back switches to the left side of the ballcarrier, and the drill is repeated.

Coaching Points: The ballcarrier takes his free hand and arm away from the ball after each blow is delivered, so that he can practice creating the two-handed carry for each blow.

Drill #5: Rapid-Fire Two-Hand Carry

This drill is performed in the same fashion as the two-hand carry drill, except that two backs face the ballcarrier, one slightly left, and the other slightly right, about 2 yards away (refer to Diagram 5-1). With the coach signaling from behind the ballcarrier, one of the other backs delivers a blow. After this blow, the ballcarrier properly switches the ball, and then takes on a blow from the second back. On each blow, the ballcarrier must properly cover the ball with his free hand

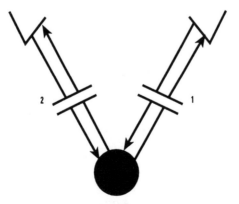

Diagram 5-1
Rapid-fire two-hand carry drill.

and arm in the two-handed carry technique. The action is repeated a set number of times in an allotted time period.

Coaching Points: The drill must not be so rapid-fire that the ballcarrier doesn't have time to reset and be ready to properly execute the two-handed carry technique.

Drill #6: Rapid-Fire Double Ball Carry

This is similar to the rapid-fire two-hand carry drill, except that the ballcarrier secures one ball in each armpit and takes on blows from both backs at the same time (refer to Diagram 5-2). The ballcarrier must attempt to drop his shoulders and absorb the blows with his shoulders, rather than his arms and hands.

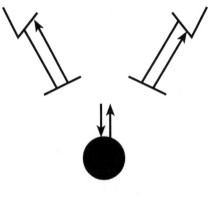

Diagram 5-2
Rapid-fire double ball carry drill.

Coaching Points: The coach must allow the ballcarrier proper time to reset after each blow. Five or six blows per man is a good allotment per set.

Drill #7: Monkey Roll

This drill is similar to the typical three-man monkey roll agility drill, except that all three backs have a football locked under one arm.

Coaching Points: Ballcarriers have a tremendous tendency to loosen the desired vise-like grip of the one-armed carry. This, of course, must be remedied. Only six or seven monkey roll repetitions should be carried out in one set, as the drill tends to disintegrate beyond that number. Disintegration must be avoided to prevent the backs from falling on each other's legs. The backs must be sure to alternate ballcarrying sides.

Drill #8: Gauntlet

In this drill, two lines of players attempt to slap, rip, punch, etc., at the ballcarrying area to jar the ball loose. Beginning the drill with a handoff adds to the effectiveness of the drill since the ballcarrier then practices the whole sequence of ball security action. The gauntlet is set up with two lines a yard-and-a-half apart with a yard between players in each line (refer to Diagram 5-3). Some of the players may utilize hand-bags to slam the ballcarrier both high and low, to disturb his ball security efforts. The ballcarrier must attempt to dash through the gauntlet as fast and powerfully as possible, while executing proper ball security techniques.

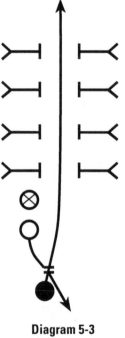

Diagram 5-3
Gauntlet drill.

Coaching Points: The ballcarrier must drive up and through the gauntlet by arching his back. He must also be sure to pump his knees high to help maintain balance. This drill also practices other facets of ballcarrying. Often in unit and team drills and practice, only one set of backs are utilized at a time. The backs who are waiting can put this extra time to good use by working on two of the ball security drills: the ball iso drill, and the changing the ball drill. A simple practice rule says, "If you're not in the team work, scrimmage, etc., you must have a ball in your hand, working the Ball Iso or Changing the Ball." For extra benefit, add the Arm Wrestling Drill. A coach can sneak up on a back in between the plays being run and attempt to punch, rip, or slap the ball out of the waiting back's arm. If the ball isn't secure and pops out, a sanction such as ten push-ups or ten up-downs can be assigned to reinforce emphasis on ball security.

Additional ball security emphasis can be gained by insisting that proper ball security techniques be carried out all throughout practice. If a back carries a ball from one practice area to another, he must do it with "no air," elbow wrapped around and under the ball, fingers covering the tip of the ball, etc. After a scrimmage, team work, or timing period execution, a back can be expected to execute proper ball security techniques all the way back to the huddle. Such extra practice work makes for more complete and efficient use of every available practice minute. In addition, concentrated emphasis is embedded in the minds of those who most need it—the players. Far too often a coach says he lacks sufficient time to work on such drills or details. These little tricks can produce far more efficient and effective practice time.

FAKING TECHNIQUES

Effective backfield faking can greatly enhance backfield performance. An unblocked defensive tackle may be influenced to tackle a faking diveback. A linebacker who steps up to honor a diveback's fake on a play-action pass or option play may take himself out of the play. What is often so beneficial about faking action is that as little as one step can eliminate defenders from the play without blocking them. A linebacker may be unable to reach the hook-curl zone on a pass drop and leave a curling flanker uncovered because of a well-executed fake, or be unable to get to the perimeter to help defense an option play.

Two common problems occur with backfield faking. Sometimes it is overlooked, not receiving enough attention from the coaches. Sometimes the backs overexaggerate the faking action, rendering it ineffective. Either situation is detrimental to effective backfield execution.

The key to effective backfield faking is to simply make the faking action look like a normal play execution. The action must not be exaggerated, or it reveals the fake. If a quarterback holds the ball up in the air as he drops back to execute a draw handoff, he may as well yell "Draw!" to the defense, because his action gives the defense a definite key to the play.

Each appropriate fake depends on the design of the offensive play. The speed of a play's execution may require the quarterback to give less of a fake. An optimal handoff fake exists for each play, either one- or two-handed.

A two-handed fake of a handoff by the quarterback provides the best opportunity to influence defenders, because the ball is placed in the faking back's pouch and ridden toward the line of scrimmage until the final point where the quarterback must withdraw the ball. Such a fake best simulates the play action that the fake is trying to emulate.

The quarterback moves to the mesh point as he would on the normal handoff action that the fake is simulating. He keeps his shoulders level all through the faking action as he would in a normal handoff (refer to Figure 6-1).

The ball is extended to the faking back's pouch and is ridden along the back's course. This ride should go no farther than to the quarterback's belt buckle on the plane that the front of his body is facing. A ride farther than this will create the possibility of the faking back's hip bone interfering with the withdrawal of the ball from the back's pouch. Once the ball is ridden to the quarterback's belt buckle, it is simply drawn back to the quarterback's stomach—his third hand. Dive faking on option plays is a prime example of the importance of never faking beyond the quarterback's belt buckle, as seen in Figure 6-1, which shows a halfback dive fake.

Ball in pouch

Ridden to belt buckle

Drawn back to stomach

Figure 6-1
Two-handed fake action by the QB.

70

Many coaches prefer a one-handed handoff fake, feeling it better protects the ball, and helps facilitate quicker movement into the real play after the fake. One-handed fakes are most commonly used on play-action passes, to help facilitate the necessary drop-back action to set up for delivery of the pass.

On a one-handed handoff, the quarterback positions the ball just above the junction at the top of his leg and the bottom of his stomach (refer to Figure 6-2). Actually, the ball sits on the soft bottom of his stomach in order to not interfere with the legs' movement. The quarterback must be sure the ball does not rest on his hip bone, because it will not be well protected if he is hit from behind. The soft surface of his stomach helps absorb the shock of a hit, where the hard bone would tend to aid the ball's being jarred loose.

The free hand fakes the handoff into the faking back's pouch. The hand can actually ride in the pouch as long as the body movement away from the mesh point will allow. The quarterback can actually initiate his movement away from the mesh point as soon as the faking back clears the quarterback's intended path.

Two common errors on the one-handed handoff fake must be avoided by the quarterback. First, the quarterback must not raise his upper body too high, as the one-handed fake action will often cause him to do. He must keep his shoulders as level as possible to the initial level of his shoulders in his pre-snap stance. Second, he must be sure to execute a good one-handed ride with the faker's pouch, and not pull out to quickly in his eagerness to carry out the rest of the play's action.

QUARTERBACK PASS-ACTION FAKING

The quarterback's action of faking a pass for such plays as a draw or a screen is simply executed by carrying out his normal drop-back or sprint-out action, and by not overexaggerating the fake. The ball is carried as in a normal pass-drop action, in front of the chest to the side of the carry. The ball must not be held up high for the defense to see, as this obviousness is only a dead giveaway to the defense that the play is a screen or a draw. One of the best things the quarterback can do to influence pass-drop action by the defenders is to "look off." Looking off refers to the fact that the quarterback looks into the secondary as long as he can, as if he were reading the secondary's drop movements and looking for his receivers. This action will often influence the linebackers and deep backs to drop off quickly into pass coverage, which then sets up the draw or the screen.

On some running plays, the quarterback may fake a pass action after handing the ball off. This requires some coaching points. First, the quarterback can initially help influence defenders to honor his fake by accelerating at top speed from the handoff mesh. A real burst of speed can often cause enough concern to hold a defender in his alignment, or even force him to flow with the

**Positioning of ball
on soft of stomach**

One-hand fake

One-hand ride

**Figure 6-2
One-handed fake action by the QB.**

acceleration. Second, the quarterback must attempt to hide his hands as they fake his carry of the ball, by slightly turning his upper torso away from the line of scrimmage as if to hide his hands with the back of his shoulder. Third, the quarterback must keep his head up and attempt to look the linebackers and secondary defenders off. Such positioning of the upper torso and hands, plus a sprinting acceleration toward the launch point of the fake pass play, will do much to cause concern to the defense. Such actions by the quarterback fake a bootleg-type action.

Figure 6-3
Quarterback pass fake.

OTHER QUARTERBACK FAKING ACTION

Other faking actions exist that a quarterback might have to carry out in the execution of his particular offense. The key concept, again, is that the faking actions must closely approximate the actions of a real play. Exaggeration must be avoided. Faking a toss or a quick-pitch are prime examples. The quarterback must carry his body in the same way and on the same plane as if he were actually delivering the ball. All toss or quick-pitch actions should be executed, such as eye concentration, follow-through, etc. The ball must not be lifted high to exaggerate the fake, as this will only create a key for the defense that the action is a fake.

Another common quarterback fake is executing an option fake of the keep-pitch key. The faking concepts are identical. Thus, the quarterback accelerates from the handoff mesh at top speed, stares at the keep-pitch key defender, and brings his hands to the normal pitch position. Even though the defender may quickly see that the quarterback does not have the ball, this action will usually delay him long enough to prevent, or at least slow, his pursuit of the ballcarrier. In addition, the option fake action will often force interior defender pursuit, further helping to influence defenders away from the ballcarrier.

A concentrated effort on coordinating movement of the free hands once a handoff has been made is also a key action in helping to influence defenders to the faking action. This concept was thoroughly discussed in Chapter 4 in the explanation of the quarterback handoff technique.

Whatever the faking action is, the quarterback must be sure to carry out his faking assignment, and not stop to watch the ballcarrier. Nothing provides a better defensive key than for the quarterback to discontinue his faking action and point out the ballcarrier to the defense by watching him run.

RUNNING BACK FAKE OF HANDOFF

The running backs execute the handoff fake in the same manner as they would execute an actual handoff. The "faking" back creates a normal handoff pouch. The bottom hand is palm up, just off the belt buckle, with the fingers and thumb hyper-extended down toward the ground. The "V"-shaped carry of the arms allows for the ball to be freely placed in the faker's pouch and withdrawn without interference.

To further facilitate noninterference with the quarterback's faking action, the back should hold his arm position for a split second longer than he would if he were actually receiving the handoff. Actually, he should wait until he feels the ball being withdrawn from his pouch before he begins to fold over the faking action.

The actual faking action simply has the back fold his arms together to form the "V"-shaped pouch position, so the hand of his top arm folds underneath the elbow of the bottom arm. His hands are flatly pressed against the side of the rib cage, while his arms press against his stomach. As a result of the folding action, both hands are hidden underneath both elbows. This folding action enables the fake to create as much hand and arm surface over the pouch as possible, which helps hide the fact of whether or not the ball is in the pouch. This action is diametrically opposed to a hard clamping action of both arms, which does little to sell a fake, and actually gives the defender a key to read, since the clamping action is not used to receive a handoff.

Two important concepts are tied in with the folding of the arms in the faking action. First, hunching over the faking action with the back's head down is a dead giveaway the back doesn't have the ball, because a ballcarrier would never run in this hunched position. The back must keep his head up and eyes open, as if he were looking for daylight to carry the ball to. Second, the back must accelerate at top speed, just as he would if he were carrying the ball. An explosive action from the fake mesh point, with the arms correctly folded and the head up, is what will sell the fake and force commitment to the faking action by the defenders.

OTHER RUNNING BACK FAKING ACTIONS

The key for other run faking actions coincides with the key for faking in general. Carry out execution of all the normal actions being faked, accelerate, and do not exaggerate actions that reveal the fake. In faking the pitch or toss reception, for example, the back must not throw his arms up, or perform any other type of exaggerated action. Instead, the back must accelerate into his proper course, form his normal basket carry with his hands, and stare at the quarterback's hands as if the ball were actually to be released. This action mirrors identically the normal pitch action and creates the best chance of selling the fake, thereby holding the defenders in a position in which they cannot pursue the actual ballcarrier.

BACKFIELD FAKING PRACTICE AND DRILLS

Numerous opportunities exist for practice and coaching backfield faking all throughout a practice session. Every time a play is run in timing drills, unit work, team work, scrimmages, and even individual drills, some type of diversion or faking assignment involving either the quarterbacks or the running backs almost always occurs. A poorly executed dive fake on a predetermined keep-pitch option offers the coach an opportunity to correct, teach, and coach a vital and important facet of offensive execution.

Drilling fake action is usually coordinated with the drilling of other actions. This approach helps combine faking into a coordinated pattern of psychomotor skill development, along with other skills that go hand-in-hand with faking actions. Thus, quarterback option faking is better combined with the dive handoff action from which it develops. This combination of faking action in a drill with other associated skills not only helps create a game-like practice situation, it also helps create efficient use of practice time.

Drill #1: Handoff Pouch and Fake

This drill is like the handoff pouch and reception drill discussed in Chapter 4, except that the backs execute a folding fake action rather than receiving a handoff.

Coaching Points: The coach watches the back for the folding, pressing the stomach action, with the back's hands pressed to the sides of his rib cage underneath his elbows. All backs must keep their heads up and eyes looking for daylight. The coach must be sure they don't exaggerate the action with either a harsh clamping action or by hunching over.

Drill #2: Handoff Pouch and Fake Circle Drill

This is actually nothing more than the handoff pouch and reception drill from Chapter 4, except that the backs execute their folding fake instead of receiving the handoff.

Coaching Points: Same as for the handoff pouch and fake drill.

AUTHOR'S NOTE

Several other drills exist that also practice faking action along with other skill actions. The timing drill and the breakdown drill in Chapter 4, for example, afford the coach an opportunity to drill faking on specific plays, while allowing for a maximum number of repetitions. A fun type of challenge can be added to this drill by telling the quarterback to run any play of a particular continuous series (e.g., the sprint-draw, or the sprint-draw play-action sprint-out pass of the sprint-draw series) without the coach's knowing what the particular play is. The coach stands in front of the drill approximately 10 yards away and rates how well the play is disguised and how well the faking was executed. In other words, how well does the faking action "fool the coach"? In this manner, not only are the play and subsequent faking practiced, but, in addition, a firm understanding is developed of the concept of the relationships between the similar actions of a specific play series.

CHAPTER 7

RUNNING TECHNIQUES AND FUNDAMENTALS

Running with the football, or ballcarrying, is often under-coached. All coaches would love to have the great natural runner who seems to take care of the ballcarrying skills all by himself. However, such running backs are by far the exception rather than the rule. Far more often, the coach must deal with the less-than-super back who needs to work as hard to develop his skills as any other player on the field.

As discussed in Chapter 3, an explosive stance and an explosive take-off are paramount to effective ballcarrying. A back who hits a hole too slowly may find that hole closing as he approaches it. A back who doesn't hit the hole in a low, powerfully gathered stance may find he lacks the drive and power to blast for the extra yard needed for a first down. A slow take-off on a sweep may result in a back is not being able to turn the corner, because the defense is given the time to pursue to the corner and run the play down.

In addition to explosive stance and take-off, two other important factors are essential to effective ballcarrying—acceleration through an opening and open-field running. Acceleration through an opening can be divided into three separate techniques: the dive, the freeze, and the end run.

THE DIVE CONCEPT

The term "dive" refers to a ballcarrier's running with the ball directly off the blocking scheme without a lead or isolation blocker in front of him. This technique is used on such plays as a basic dive, a cutback dive, a draw, a sprint-draw, or some type of counter-dive or cross-buck. The dive technique is based on the ballcarrier's hitting the landmark as quickly and explosively as possible, and breaking tightly north-south off the line's blocking scheme, in an effort to accelerate through the daylight opening to burst into the secondary.

By hitting the landmark, or point of attack, as quickly and explosively as possible, the back can create a running head start and burst through the opening created by the blocking scheme as it develops. Far too many backs ease toward the line, waiting to see the daylight develop before they start to explode, but this usually results in the daylight closing up as they approach. Instead, the ballcarrier must already be at or near top speed as he approaches the line of scrimmage, so he has the speed and momentum to explode through the hole while it exists. He must realize that limits exist as to how long the linemen can hold their blocks. The whole concept of the dive play is a quick opening and an explosive burst through that daylight.

If no hole develops, explosive running becomes important in another way, because the ballcarrier will be at maximum speed and power when he hits the line, and can lower his shoulder and blast out yardage on his own. In a sense, he then becomes his own blocker, and so must hit with full speed and full power.

Remember that the term "*landmark*" signifies the play's point of attack. The landmark determines the linemen's blocking scheme, as well as the point to which the ballcarrier explodes on his take-off to provide a consistent mesh point for the quarterback-ballcarrier exchange. After the exchange, the ballcarrier can break from his landmark course and adjust his path to best accelerate through any daylight that may develop. The break to daylight must not, however, start until *after* a perfect handoff at the designated mesh point.

The design of a run play, and its landmark, may produce a basic dive concept, with the diveback exploding toward one specific point, such as the hip of a guard, butt of a tackle, etc. On the other hand, the run play may produce a more complex dive concept, such as breaking to daylight anywhere from inside a kick-out block all the way to the back side, as in a sprint-draw play. These two extreme uses of the dive concept are shown in Diagram 7-1, with a predetermined outside veer dive from a split backfield alignment and an "I" formation sprint-draw.

Some coaches believe that a deepened backfield alignment, as in an "I" formation, is designed for a slow-hitting action by the ballcarrier so he can better read the blocking scheme and break to daylight. However, such a conclusion is only partially correct. Actually, the deepened alignment of the ballcarrier is designed for a better sense of timing of the blocking scheme and the ballcarrier's approach to the line of scrimmage. The ballcarrier is better able to read the blocking and the resulting daylight. In addition, the deepened alignment permits him to get a strong running start, so he can hit the landmark as quickly and explosively as possible, bursting through the daylight and exploding into the secondary.

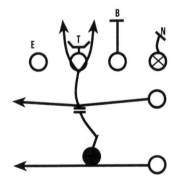 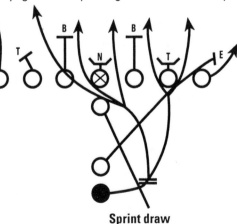

Predetermined outside veer dive   Sprint draw

Diagram 7-1
Extreme examples of the dive concept run path possibilities.

Reading the daylight produced by the blocking scheme actually starts in the preset and set stance prior to the snap of the ball. By peering ahead and using peripheral vision, the ballcarrier observes the defensive alignment, determines whose block to read, determines the possible presnap defensive adjustments, and possibly how blocking schemes will develop. Of course, these presnap reads must be adjusted by observing blocking calls and defensive movements after the snap (refer to Diagram 7-2).

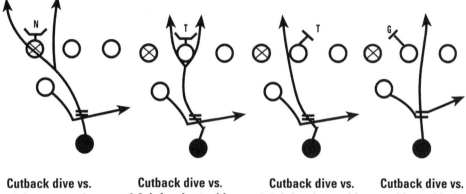

| Cutback dive vs. 5-2 noseguard | Cutback dive vs. 4-3 defensive tackle | Cutback dive vs. 4-4 defensive tackle | Cutback dive vs. wide-tackle 6 defensive guard |

Diagram 7-2
Preset reads to help determine running action.

The cutback dive, depending on the design of the offense, is usually predicated on the ballcarrier's breaking off the block of the first covered lineman from the center to the play side, in an attempt to slow pursuit by the middle interior defender(s). The cutback dive is especially effective when defenders are over-pursuing and getting to the perimeter quickly, thereby providing extra defenders against perimeter runs. Thus, the determination of how the defenders are aligned helps indicate how the ballcarrier may have to cut. A 3-4 noseguard or a 4-3 defensive tackle could determine a break to either side. A 4-4 defensive tackle *usually* means an inside cut, and a defensive tackle aligned on a guard's inside eye usually means an outside cut.

Remember, these are only *general indications*. If the 4-4 tackle happens to take an inside charge, forcing the guard to block him inside, the ballcarrier should, of course, break to the outside of the block. The same would be true for a wide-tackle six defensive tackle aligned on the guard's inside eye taking an outside charge. If the offensive guard is forced to block him to the outside, the ballcarrier will have to break to daylight inside of the guard's block (refer to Diagram 7-3).

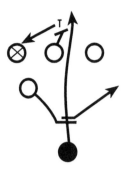 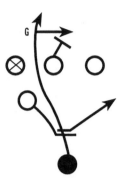

Cutting outside of 4-4 tackle's inside charge on cutback dive action

Cutting inside of wide-tackle 6 tackle's outside dive action

Diagram 7-3
Examples of how defensive alignment may only be an indicator of defensive action.

Examples of how the line blocking calls and/or blocking schemes may affect the path of the ballcarrier are shown in Diagram 7-4. The split-backfield halfback, upon hearing a call by the guard or tackle for a combo block, knows that his course will definitely be to the outside of the scheme. The "I" or wishbone formation fullback, hearing a call for a fold block, knows he must break initially outside of the tackle's down block, and then secondly break off the guard's fold block on the linebacker.

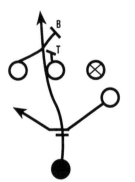 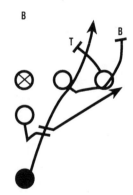

Dive with combo block vs. 4-4 look

Dive with fold block vs. 4-3 college look

Diagram 7-4
Ballcarrier path determined by blocking scheme.

Once the ballcarrier reads the blocking of the blockers, he must break to daylight off the blocks as quickly and tightly as possible. Breaking upfield tightly off a block ensures north-south running, thereby going for the goal line as directly as possible. Lateral distance to the left or right of a block wastes time getting through the daylight toward the goal line. In addition, wasted time getting to and through the daylight allows extra time for the defenders to catch the ballcarrier. An example of this concept is shown in Diagram 7-5 for an "I" formation fullback dive, in which the fullback breaks off the guard's block on an even-defense defensive tackle.

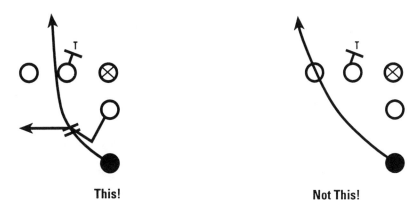

This!   **Not This!**

Diagram 7-5
Tight north-south running off the blocking action.

All lateral movement compromises the ballcarrier's north-south advance toward the goal line. Remember that the shortest distance between two points is a straight line. A back should think like a skier cutting the gates as closely as possible to shave every split-second off his time to beat his opponents. The slightest unnecessary lateral variance can allow the defenders an extra split second to catch the ballcarrier's ankle and trip him up.

It is important to emphasize that after the ballcarrier's explosive take-off to hit the daylight, he should then concentrate on bursting—"exploding"—through that daylight into the secondary before the defense can close the hole. Every inch gained cuts down a defender's pursuit angle, making it more difficult for him to tackle the runner.

The technique used by the back to explode through the hole is to open up or stretch his strides as he bursts through the opening. This action is similar to a basketball guard's lengthening his strides to the bucket after he beats his man on a drive. Elongated strides help put greater distance between him and the defender, stride for stride.

On all dive concept running, remember that a good back uses his speed and power to become his own blocker if the hole is closed (i.e., no daylight), to try to make his own hole, or blow defenders back and at least grind out a few yards. The ballcarrier attempts to rip up under the shoulder pads of defensive players, much the same as executing a drive block. Key elements to success are a good base and continuing leg drive. He should buck upward, arching his back, and keeping his head up. A coaching adage—"head down and you go down"—is often true whether defenders are tackling the ballcarrier or not.

THE FREEZE TECHNIQUE

A second technique for acceleration through an opening, besides the dive technique, is the freeze technique, which is used to set up a linebacker for a block, usually a down block or an isolation block. In the freeze technique, the ballcarrier runs directly at the defender being set up, to "freeze" him. Freezing means that since the defender can't tell which way the ballcarrier is going to break, he stays fixed to a spot, often flat-footed. For the defender to commit himself to one side or the other too early could be costly, so he stays put. This situation is especially true on an isolation play run directly at a linebacker, where the ballcarrier is keyed to break opposite the attack of the linebacker and the block of the isolation blocker. Because the play is designed this way, both the ballcarrier and the isolation blocker can afford to be more aggressive, since even a less-than-perfect block will wall the linebacker off to one side or the other as the ballcarrier explodes by on the opposite side.

On the other hand, if the linebacker tries to sit and fight the blocker off, he will then have to contend with both the blocker and the runner exploding into him with maximum speed and power. The isolation play freeze action is shown in Diagram 7-6.

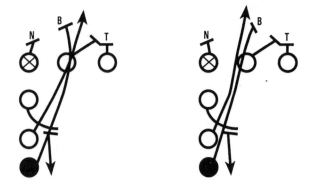

Diagram 7-6
Isolation play freeze action.

The freeze technique is also used in the trap play (refer to Diagram 7-7), where the ballcarrier explodes directly at the linebacker who will be downblocked.

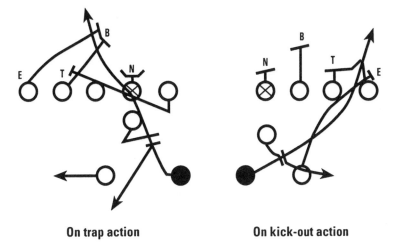

On trap action   **On kick-out action**

Diagram 7-7
Freeze technique on trap and kick-out actions.

The action of a ballcarrier to explode directly at a linebacker will freeze that linebacker in place and prevent his undesired outside pursuit, which would result if the ballcarrier were to break more widely off the trap action. A wide break by the ballcarrier would cause a wider down block by the tight end and tackle, which in turn would force the ballcarrier to run wider around the block, thereby wasting forward progress toward the end zone. Diagram 7-8 shows how failure to utilize the freeze technique on the trap play causes more undesired east-west running.

Remember, the freeze technique helps set up a block. After the blocker makes contact, all the techniques of the dive concept are then executed by the runner: breaking tightly toward the end zone off the blocking scheme, opening up and stretching his strides to explode through daylight, and becoming his own blocker if no daylight exists.

It is important to remember also that although the design of a particular play may emphasize the freeze technique, defensive actions may force the ballcarrier to revert to dive concept running. This situation is shown, for example, in Diagram 7-9, with an "I" formation isolation play in which the center is forced to drive block the noseguard to the onside, due to the noseguard's movement.

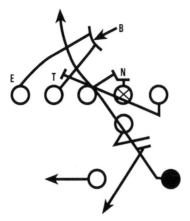

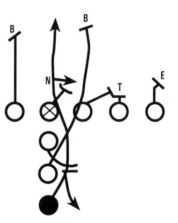

Diagram 7-8
Failure to use freeze technique
on trap play and resultant
east-west running.

Diagram 7-9
Defensive action causing
breakdown of the freeze
technique.

END-RUN TECHNIQUES

The third technique for accelerating through daylight is the end-run technique. End-run ballcarrying, whether off option, sweep, or quick-pitch action, or any other type of end-run play, also emphasizes the importance of north-south running toward the end zone. The running in all of these plays is based on outflanking the defense with blockers in order to provide a run lane up the sideline, or straight upfield inside the perimeter-support-contain defender as he is kicked-out to the sideline by a blocker.

The end-run ballcarrier's take-off (refer to the discussion of take-offs in Chapter 3) is of utmost importance, since the ballcarrier's lateral speed must beat the pursuit of the inside defenders. The runner must not stand up, waste any motion with a lateral stepping action, or carry his body loosely. Actual end-run techniques are determined by one of three end-run play designs: (1) following an arc blocker, (2) following a pulling lineman, or (3) sharply turning a hard blocked corner.

Following an arc blocker is perhaps the most demanding end-run assignment, since the combined action of the arc blocker and the ballcarrier relies so heavily on each other's individual actions. The arc blocking technique will be discussed more thoroughly in Chapter 11. For now, it must be established that the ballcarrier's run action sets up the arc block for the arc blocker. The ballcarrier is kept on an arc course until the arc block is executed (refer to Diagram 7-10). After the blocker makes contact, the ballcarrier breaks tightly upfield off the arc block.

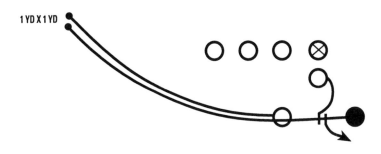

Diagram 7-10
Arc relationship between the arc blocker and a ballcarrier.

Until the arc block is executed, the ballcarrier must keep a constant one-yard by one-yard relationship with the arc blocker's outside hip. Since the blocker sets the arc-shaped route, the ballcarrier is responsible for "flying in formation," like a fighter pilot maintaining the proper distance with his lead, no matter how extreme the course set by the arc blocker.

The design of the arc block technique determines that if the ballcarrier maintains his relationship to the arc blocker, the defender will be unable to tackle the ballcarrier. If the defender makes the mistake of attempting to go under the arc blocker, the blocker simply shapes his block up sharply into the defender, as the ballcarrier breaks sharply upfield around the block and explodes north-south toward the end zone. If the defender tries to fight through the arc blocker's head, this action creates a perfect situation for the arc block delivery. Once again, the runner will be able to accelerate sharply upfield around the arc block. If the defender widens toward the sideline so much that the arc block can't create an outside run lane, or if the defender comes upfield so far that the arc block can't be executed without a dipping or bellying action, the arc blocker executes a reverse hip action, and the ballcarrier breaks sharply upfield north-south up under the block. These actions are illustrated in Diagram 7-11.

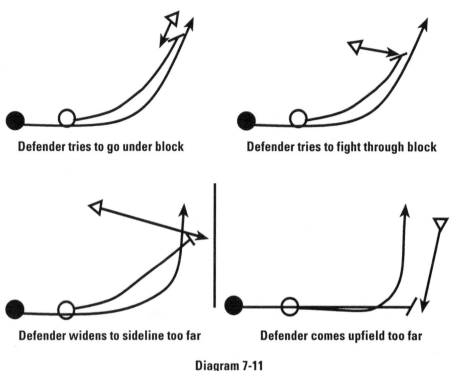

Defender tries to go under block

Defender tries to fight through block

Defender widens to sideline too far

Defender comes upfield too far

Diagram 7-11
Ballcarrier and arc block action vs. various defensive reactions.

Again, the ballcarrier must maintain the arc relationship until the block is delivered. He must stay "on the hip and never dip." Failure to do so will break down the setup of the block and enable the defender to play through the arc blocker and get to the ballcarrier.

Following a pulling lineman can also utilize the arc block concept, with the pulling lineman becoming the arc blocker, as seen in the quick-pitch play shown in Diagram 7-12. In this case, the tackle and the ballcarrier carry out the arc block reactions to various defenses (refer to Diagram 7-11).

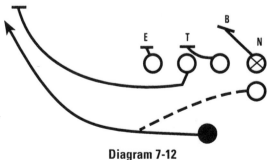

Diagram 7-12
Lineman arc block concept.

More often, however, pulling linemen are given other specific assignments, such as a kick-out of the perimeter corner-support defender, or a lead-block assignment. Both of these actions can be seen in Diagram 7-13, in a split-back pro sweep, with two guards pulling, and the blocking back load-blocking on the defensive end.

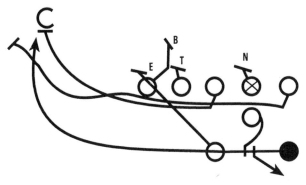

Diagram 7-13
Sweep action with pulling guards.

When the blocking scheme calls for a pulling lineman's kick-out action against the perimeter corner-support defender, the ballcarrier can help set up the block by using the freeze technique. In this case, the ballcarrier attacks upfield, directly at the defender, to freeze him in his position. Using the freeze technique puts the defender in a bind, and he'll have to play a more sitting, passive style, helping to set up an easier block for the pulling lineman.

If the pulling lineman is lead-blocking upfield, rather than having a specific kick-out assignment, the freeze technique may again be used. The ballcarrier helps put the defender in a bind by running directly at him to freeze him, helping set up the block for the pulling lineman. Although not actually within the scope of this book, it is worth mentioning that the pulling lineman must attempt more of a perimeter stalk block than any more typical aggressive lineman's run block, since the lineman will be trying to block a more nimble defender in the open field. Cross-body blocking is also an excellent alternative for pulling linemen.

On both types of pulling action, kick-out and lead, emphasis should be on the ballcarrier's north-south attack. Whether on an option play, a sweep, or a quick-pitch, the end-run play is designed mainly to get the ballcarrier around the corner and upfield as quickly as possible, to advance toward the end zone. Always remember that more lateral run action gives the defenders more time to pursue to the corner to support the perimeter defense. The purpose of an offensive play is to outflank the defense with blockers and a ballcarrier. The more straight ahead the ballcarrier explodes as he turns the corner, the more he eliminates the pursuit angles of the interior front defenders. This concept is illustrated in Diagram 7-14, where ballcarrier "A" has the defensive front outflanked and has virtually eliminated their pursuit ability, since he has passed them. Ballcarrier "B" has the defensive front outflanked, but the defenders still have excellent pursuit angles, due to the poor north-south progress of the ballcarrier.

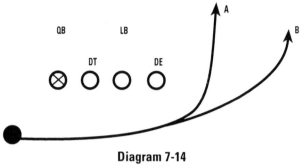

Diagram 7-14
North-south end-run ballcarrying as compared to
non-north-south end-run ballcarrying.

    North-south running is also crucial to an end-run play around a hard-blocked corner, as shown in Diagram 7-15, where immediate blocking pressure goes against the corner, usually by using a lead-back cut-down type "H" or loadblock. This play is used against an over-shifted linebacker 3-4 defense to a split-end side, where the weak-side defensive end is stacked behind the defensive tackle. The offensive tackle sets up the cut-down block for the lead blocker by slamming the defensive tackle before releasing to block the stacked defensive end. Such a hard-corner blocking attack emphasizes a total "burn" by the ballcarrier, in an effort to swing tightly around the defensive front, so as to outflank it and burst upfield north-south before defenders are able to pursue.

    The Green Bay pro sweep is another end-run action (refer to Diagram 7-16). In this play, the ballcarrier is given more of an option as to where to break in relation to the corner blocking scheme. Keyed on the block of the tight end, both the ballcarrier and the lead pulling guard read the tight end's action to determine whether they cut up inside his block or continue out around it. In either case, the ballcarrier will utilize the concepts of explosively hitting and bursting through the open daylight and quickly turning the corner toward the goal. As in the freeze technique, the ballcarrier emphasizes all the aspects of breaking tightly north-south off the blocking, and opening up or stretching his strides as he explodes.

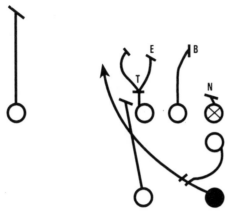

Diagram 7-15
Example of a hard-blocked corner for end-run action.

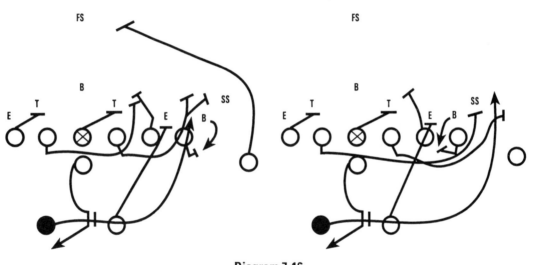

Diagram 7-16
Green Bay sweep end-run action.

OPEN-FIELD RUNNING

Many coaches feel that you can't teach a back about open-field running, that once he breaks into the open he must rely only on his natural abilities to carry him into the end zone. It is true that a talented back with great speed and good faking moves will have a definite advantage in such situations, and that only a limited number of techniques exist for avoiding a secondary defender. However, these techniques can be taught and learned to help any back run better in the open field.

One of these techniques is, again, the concept of exploding north-south toward the goal line and elongating his strides. All cutting or veering action should come off "torrid" north-south acceleration, which puts extra stress on the secondary to react quickly. This factor helps create better cutting angles for the runner, based on the defender's reactions. In addition, rapid acceleration helps to eliminate pursuit by the front defenders, who have a chance to recover and pursue if the ballcarrier hesitates or runs laterally. Thus, the more the ballcarrier stresses north-south acceleration, the fewer the number of defenders who will have a shot at him.

The major fault that must be eliminated during open-field running is the tendency to run east-west, or sideways, in an attempt to avoid secondary defenders. Although a runner may occasionally take the long route across the field and outrun his pursuers up the opposite sideline, statistics show convincingly that far more often he would have been more successful gaining yardage toward the goal line had he knifed upfield and executed any cutting or veering action off a concerted north-south effort. More often than not, lateral running only allows the defense more time to pursue and provides defenders with better pursuit angles. Thus, the ballcarrier not only has farther to run, but more defenders with which to contend.

If the ballcarrier is knifing directly upfield and finds a secondary defender directly in front of him, the freeze technique can again be employed. An early cut or veer only gives the defender a better pursuit angle and makes any further cutting or veering all the more difficult. Running directly at the defender will put him in a bind, wondering in which direction the ballcarrier will break. This forces the defender to freeze, thereby becoming more passive and possibly flat-footed. Then, as the ballcarrier is on top of the defender, he breaks or cuts sharply, and accelerates by opening up the length of his strides to put distance between himself and the defender.

The runner can set up his cut while running straight at the defender by faking with his head or upper body, "stutter stepping," using the limp-leg technique, change of pace, or any other type of faking action. Any fake will work better if the ballcarrier puts the defender in a bind first with a top-speed, north-south attack directly at him.

Another important concept that can be coached for successful open-field running is that once the ballcarrier has broken into the open, with no defender in front of him, he must run a 100-yard dash to the end zone. Nothing must detract from his speed, course, and effort—especially turning around to see where his pursuers are. Turning around accomplishes nothing, except to slow him down and give his pursuers a chance to catch him.

When the defender dives to tackle the runner from behind and makes contact with the ballcarrier's back leg area, a high-step, or stride-out action can help the runner keep from being tripped up. The runner should kick his feet out toward the goal line, reaching for the goal with his toes as his upper torso leans back slightly. This action propels his legs away from the defender's grasp and elevates his feet to avoid stubbing or being driven into the ground, and being tripped up.

At times, cutting back against the grain does have its merits. It must be executed, however, off top-speed north-south running, with tight cutting or veering actions, staying as close as possible to the straight-up-the-field line. Refer to Diagram 7-17 for an excellent example of this technique where the defender has a good pursuit angle to hem the ballcarrier into the sideline.

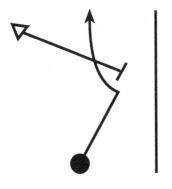

Diagram 7-17
Open field cutting across the grain.

Again, the success of the cutback action is the heavy initial north-south run threat up the sideline to force the defender to "sell out" on his pursuit effort. Thus, the defender's over-commitment, plus a tight north-south cut behind the defender to the goal line, helps this across-the-grain, tight cutting action to be of tremendous value.

If the ballcarrier is hemmed into the sideline and sees no chance to cut back across the grain, due to the defender's pursuit angle, or a number of defenders closing in, he should simply attempt to drive-block himself up the sideline as far as he can get. Drive blocking means that he lowers his inside shoulder and attempts to drive up under the shoulder pads of his would-be tackler in order to blast himself forward for positive yardage. Maximum follow-through with powerful leg drive will help maximize the gain.

Another widely used open-field running technique is spinning out. Since many situations exist where the spin-out can be effectively utilized, it will have its own section later in this chapter.

DIVE-JUMP TECHNIQUE

The technique of jumping over a pileup of blockers and defenders to gain short yardage needed for a touchdown or first down involves some specific techniques.

Initially, the quarterback must make the handoff as deep as possible to enable the ballcarrier time to pick his jump spot and gather his feet, so he can launch himself over the pileup.

The ballcarrier explodes to the line of scrimmage at top speed to get a running head start. At approximately a yard to a yard-and-a-half in front of the pileup, he gathers his feet closely together, so he can execute a two-footed running broad jump at maximum speed and power. All effort is concentrated into thrusting his upper torso—which is cradling the ball securely—forward to carry the ball far enough to gain the necessary first down yardage, or to cross the goal line. On his approach, the ballcarrier must locate the best spot to propel his body forward, so that he can adjust both the launch point and the forward thrust of his body toward an open area. In addition, he must be sure to stay as parallel to the ground as possible as he flies over the pile, to create the least possible surface for a linebacker to hit.

The ballcarrier must be careful, when striving for needed first down yardage, that he does not extend the ball out beyond his body, thereby risking poor ball security. The ball must be firmly tucked away, so that a fumble does not occur upon contact, unless, of course, this effort extends the ball across the goal line. The dive-jump technique, or actually the drill used to perfect it, is shown in Figure 7-1.

DIVE-SQUEEZE TECHNIQUE

The dive-squeeze technique is another technique that can be used to blast for needed first-down yardage, or to crash the plane of the goal line. It can be utilized straight forward, slanting laterally, or in a corner-run play to cross inside the corner flag of the end zone. These situations are the only times that the ballcarrier lunges out to gain yardage instead of concentrating on a north-south leg drive follow-through.

In the dive-squeeze, the ballcarrier attempts to squeeze himself between two defenders, as shown in Figure 7-2, or between a defender and the end zone flag by dropping one shoulder, usually the inside shoulder, to turn the plane of his shoulders nearly perpendicular to the ground, or parallel to the crack between defenders, so that he can knife through the crack between the defenders. This position narrows the contact surface between his shoulder pads and the defender's bodies, giving the diving ballcarrier more power, and the defenders less. The ballcarrier should think of his shoulders as a wedge opening up a crack between defenders.

Approach to launch point   **Gathering of the feet**

Launch of the body

Figure 7-1
Dive-jump technique.

93

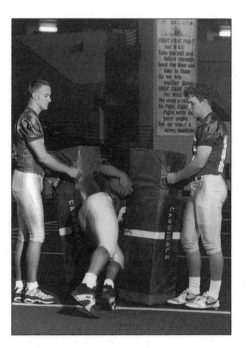

Figure 7-2
Dive-squeeze technique between two defenders.

SPINNING-OUT TECHNIQUE

Many situations exist in which a ballcarrier finds he cannot drive forward due to a pileup of blockers and/or defenders. However, he may see, feel, or sense daylight to one side or the other. A similar situation exists when the runner's progress is stopped by a single defender whose failure to wrap the ballcarrier up with his arms enables the runner to break away from the would-be tackler by spinning away from him.

The secret to performing a successful spinning-out technique is a tight north-south spin in which the ballcarrier leans on the defender, or arches his back against the defender, as he rolls off, or spins out, in an effort to continue his thrust straight forward. This movement prevents any sort of looping action that puts lateral or backward distance between the ballcarrier and the defender, thereby giving the defender time and a pursuit angle that would allow him to recover and resume pursuit.

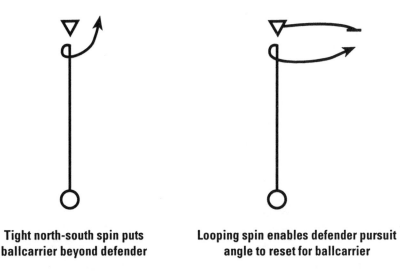

**Tight north-south spin puts
ballcarrier beyond defender**

**Looping spin enables defender pursuit
angle to reset for ballcarrier**

**Diagram 7-18
Proper execution of spinning-out technique.**

By rolling off the defender tightly, the ballcarrier will separate from the defender upfield, beyond the defender's alignment, and closer to the goal line, where he again creates an opportunity to accelerate to daylight, and a possible touchdown.

The coach must be sure that the backs don't tangle up their feet as they spin but maintain good foot balance and agility. Proper opening up, or elongation of the ballcarrier's strides, will enable him to reduce the defender's ability to pursue from behind. Diagram 7-18 illustrates the difference between a proper tight spin-out and an improper looping spin. The proper north-south, upfield spin-out is also shown in Figure 7-3.

THE STUMBLE TECHNIQUE

The stumble technique helps the ballcarrier regain his balance when he stumbles, instead of falling. The runner simply uses his free hand to break his fall by placing it on the ground, giving him a quick, stabilizing three-point stance. From the stabilized position, the ballcarrier must buck his head up, arch his back, and thrust out his chest. He also tries to pump his knees up high to help get his feet back up under him. Figure 7-4 shows the proper stumble technique.

DRAGGING OR CARRYING A DEFENDER

Dragging or carrying a defender is a skill that requires coaching attention and practice. Far too often a ballcarrier yields and is pulled down too quickly by a defender, when he could have driven for the extra yard or two that might have produced a crucial first down or a touchdown.

Forward motion stopped　　　　　　　**Tight north-south spin
arching of back on defender**

Forward thrust north-south and an opening up of the stride

**Figure 7-3
The spin out technique.**

96

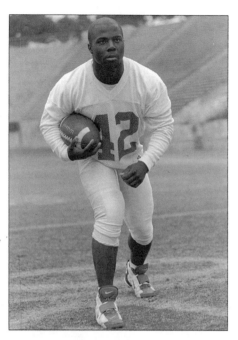

Hand breaks fall

**Head is bucked, back is arched, and
chest is thrown out**

Knees are pumped high to get feet under ballcarrier

**Figure 7-4
The stumble technique.**

Dragging or carrying the defender involves two major coaching points. First, the ballcarrier must maintain a good base as he takes short, choppy (but powerful) steps forward, while keeping his body low and powerfully gathered, and churning for north-south yardage. Forward body lean and high knee pumping actions are paramount to the success of this effort.

Second, the ballcarrier must be sure not to swing the ball loosely or away from his body as he churns his legs. The ball must be tucked securely into the armpit vise. Ball security is often a common problem during hard pumping, leg churning action, thereby creating a significant risk of a fumble.

BALLCARRYING PRACTICE AND DRILLS

Ballcarrying practice and drills are often the highlights of practice for the backs. Side exercises are usually fun type drills, since they are associated with what backs like to do most—run with the football. The coach, however, is often caught in a dilemma between which drills are game-like and which are artificial. He must keep in mind whether a drill helps practice a skill or skills, which the backs need to execute offensive assignments. If the drill does that, it is useful.

Drill #1: Dive

The dive drill is an excellent means of helping to develop north-south running, tight veering or cutting off the blocking scheme, and proper acceleration to burst through the hole and into the secondary. It is best executed utilizing a quarterback for a quarterback-ballcarrier exchange and a proper play design, so that the back can execute his dive or freeze technique in more of a game-like context. The drill pits an offensive lineman against a defensive lineman or linebacker (refer to Diagram 7-19). The back explodes behind the lineman and executes his proper running action off the lineman's block. Two cones are placed on the ground approximately two yards to each side of the blocker to act as hole markers, so the back doesn't cut too wide and too far away from the defender. This drill is designed to force the ballcarrier to utilize a shoulder drive technique if the defender is not properly blocked.

Coaching Points: The drill can be executed off any dive-running action (e.g., sprint-draw, isolation, etc.) It is also an excellent drill for offensive and defensive linemen and linebackers. The quarterback should be sure to alternate his handoffs to both sides, so the back cuts off both left-and right-handed receptions of the handoff.

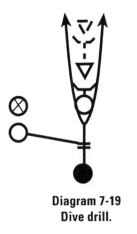

Diagram 7-19
Dive drill.

Drill #2: Nutcracker

The nutcracker drill is similar to the dive drill, except that it uses three blockers and three defenders. Two or three backs can line up behind the quarterback. However, only the back designated as the ballcarrier executes the drill.
The drill is run into a rectangle five yards wide and 10 yards deep (refer to Diagram 7-20). The offense has three downs to get the ball through this rectangle and past the far yard line. The coach designates the ballcarrier who dives straight ahead if he is aligned behind one of the outside linemen, or to one side or the other of the center, as designated by the coach, if he is the back stacked behind the quarterback. The quarterback may also be designated as the ballcarrier. The designated ballcarrier simply executes all the fundamentals of the dive concept to get past the far yard line.

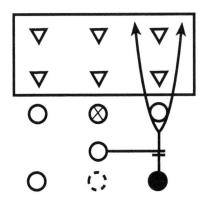

Diagram 7-20
Nutcracker drill.

Coaching Points: The defenders may be aligned in a variety of defensive sets in order to give specific defensive looks. This is a good competition type drill, pitting offense against defense. As in the dive drill, there are numerous benefits for all players involved.

Drill #3: Sideline

The sideline drill helps develop the skills of ripping explosively up the sideline and using the inside forearm to ward off blows from the simulated defenders. Three defenders position themselves with air bags two to three yards from the sideline (refer to Diagram 7-21). The ballcarrier takes a toss, quick-pitch, or option-pitch, and breaks up the sideline, simulating an end run. The three defenders attempt to slam the ballcarrier out-of-bounds.

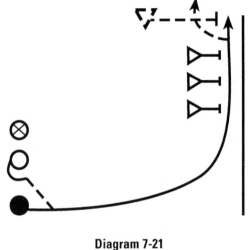

Diagram 7-21
Sideline drill.

Coaching Points: The ballcarrier must secure the ball underneath his outside arm. He must drive up through the air bags by arching his back, slamming up through the bags with his free shoulder, and using a forearm lift to help shed the bags. Proper pumping knee action and foot base are needed to help maintain his balance. An extra defender, the dotted triangle in Diagram 7-21, can be added to the drill to occasionally attack the ballcarrier from a sharp frontal angle as he passes the initial three defenders in order to give the ballcarrier the opportunity to practice the technique of cutting across the grain.

Drill #4: Flag

The flag drill helps develop the dive squeeze technique, as well as the ability to get into the end zone inside the corner flag. Two large dummies are placed at the flag, as shown in Diagram 7-22. One is positioned two yards straight out on a 45-degree angle, while the other is set down about a half-yard from the goal line. The dummies are held by extra ballcarriers about a yard apart. The ballcarrier takes some type of end-run or off-tackle ball exchange from the quarterback and uses a low, powerful, lunging drive—combined with the squeeze technique—to crash between the dummies and into the end zone in front of the flag. The dummies' holders jam the ballcarrier as hard as possible in an attempt to prevent him from reaching the end zone.

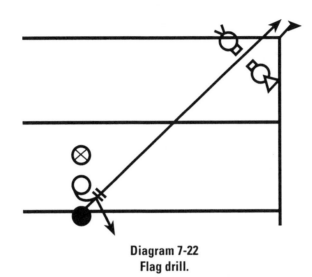

Diagram 7-22
Flag drill.

Coaching Points: The coach must check to see that the ballcarrier covers the ball with his free hand and arm upon contact. The aiming point of the dive is slightly inside the flag, to allow for the defender's lateral thrust. The ballcarrier attempts to blast out low, as if ripping through the defenders' legs, rather than through the bulk of their upper torsos.

Drill #5: Dive Squeeze

The dive squeeze drill is executed in a similar fashion to the flag drill, except that the ballcarrier blasts straight into the end zone. The bag holders hold the heavy dummies on the 1-1/2 yard line, as shown in Diagram 7-23, and do everything possible on the jamming action to prevent the ballcarrier from reaching the end zone. This technique is also shown in Figure 7-2.

Coaching Points: Turning the shoulders so they are perpendicular to the ground is paramount to success in the squeeze dive. This action lessens the surface area of the ballcarrier's shoulders that contacts the defenders, similar to a wedge driving through the crack between defenders.

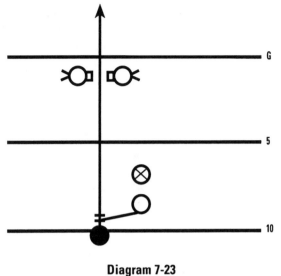

Diagram 7-23
Dive squeeze drill.

Drill #6: Dive Jump

The dive jump drill practices the skill of diving over a pileup of blockers and defenders. It necessitates a quarterback to help the run develop properly from a deep handoff. All the techniques of an exploding head start toward the opening, gathering the feet a yard to a yard-and-a-half in front of the pileup, a powerful two-footed broad-jump type action, and a powerful thrusting of the upper torso with the ball securely tucked away, are emphasized. The drill is set up by standing four or five tall dummies in front of a high-jump pit. The ballcarrier simply adjusts his approach to the "pileup" of bags and launches himself over the top. Placing the bags directly in front of the goal line gives the ballcarrier a target spot to cross over for the touchdown or first down. The drill is shown in Diagram 7-24 and Figure 7-1.

Diagram 7-24
Dive jump drill.

Coaching Points: The coach must be sure to practice all of the various types of handoffs used for the dive jump technique, and that the ballcarrier approaches the launch point from whatever angles the various plays would dictate.

Drill #7: Seven-Yard Line

The seven-yard line drill is set up similarly to the flag drill (refer to Diagram 7-25). Its purpose is to check whether the ballcarrier is maintaining proper drive and follow-through after he makes explosive contact into the two bags, instead of just lunging without a proper leg-drive follow-through. After taking the handoff from the quarterback, the ballcarrier attempts to blast through the bags, and yet retain enough balance to continue into the end zone. The players holding the heavy bags attempt to jam the ballcarrier to prevent his forward motion.

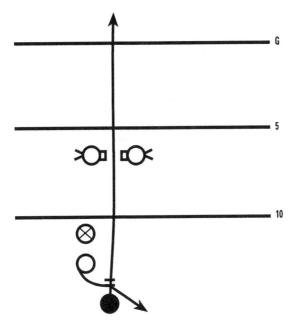

Diagram 7-25
Seven-yard line drill.

Coaching Points: The ballcarrier must cover the ball with his free arm and hand to provide extra ball security just before he makes contact. He must drive up through the dummies by arching his back and maintaining good knee pumping action to help maintain good foot balance. Occasionally, the coach signals the bag holders to fake the jamming action, and instead, to offer no resistance at all, to see if the ballcarrier is over-extending himself, causing him to fall on his face instead of continuing into the end zone.

Drill #8: Burma Road

The Burma road drill helps the backs develop the spinning-out technique. Held by other backs, four bags are placed like slalom gates, five yards wide and five yards deep (refer to Diagram 7-26). The ballcarrier attacks the first bag, delivering a shoulder drive blow with his inside shoulder, then executes a spin-out move to the inside. He then repeats the action three more times against the remaining bags.

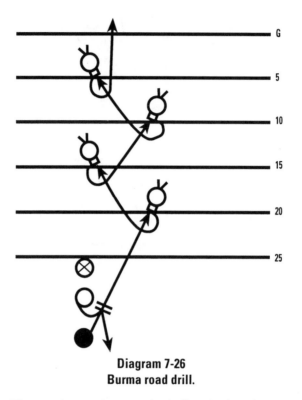

Diagram 7-26
Burma road drill.

Coaching Points: The coach must be sure the ballcarrier is using a proper shoulder drive blow, while arching his back and maintaining good foot balance. The ballcarrier should spin off the bag tightly north-south. Good foot balance and agility are important so that the ballcarrier's feet do not get tangled up.

Drill #9: Stumble

The stumble drill is designed to develop the stumble technique, which helps the ballcarrier to regain his balance when he is stumbling and falling (refer to Diagram 7-27). The drill helps create the stumbling situation by having each ballcarrier place the palm of his hand on the first yard line after a 5-yard running start. This action will cause the ballcarriers to stumble. They then execute the proper

104

stumble technique actions—buck the head up, arch the back, stick out the chest, and pump the knees to get their feet under them. Next, each ballcarrier switches the ball to his opposite arm and repeats the action with the opposite hand on the next yard line. In all, four repetitions are performed.

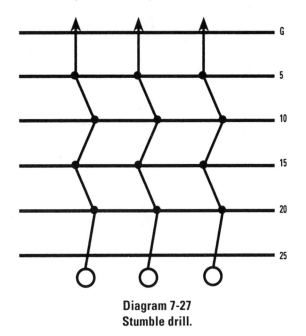

Diagram 7-27
Stumble drill.

Coaching Points: The ballcarriers must touch the palms of their hands to the yard markers, so that they stumble. The drill will be ineffective if they touch the yard lines with their fingertips and do not stumble.

Drill #10: Drag

The drag drill helps ballcarriers develop the proper techniques for driving into the end zone while dragging a defender: proper body lean, high knee pumping action, proper foot base, and good ball security. The ballcarriers, with other backs grasping around their waists to simulate tacklers, simply drive for 10 yards into the end zone (refer to Diagram 7-28).

Coaching Points: The backs simulating tacklers must attempt to be as difficult an impediment to the ballcarriers as possible.

105

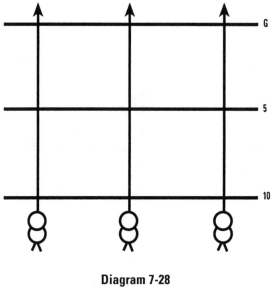

Diagram 7-28
Drag drill.

Drill #11: Carry

The carry drill is executed in exactly the same manner as the drag drill, except that the ballcarrier has the simulated tackler draped over his shoulder, as if the tackler had jumped on his back. As in the drag drill, the simulated tackler attempts to make the ballcarrier's progress into the end zone as difficult as possible.

Drill #12: Open Field Running

The open field running drill is set up by creating a 25-yard-by-25-yard square with cones. A secondary defender is placed in position A, B, or C (refer to Diagram 7-29). The ballcarrier is placed in position I, II, or III. Both the ballcarrier's and defender's alignments are continually alternated, to create all the various pursuit angles the ballcarrier might face. Upon the coach's signal, the ballcarrier attempts to utilize his open-field running skills to cross the opposite line. Simultaneously, the defender attempts to stop the ballcarrier. The drill can be run anywhere from full-tackle to two-hand touch, depending on the purpose of the drill.

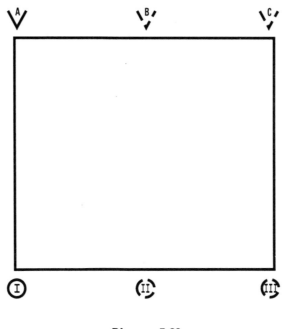

Diagram 7-29
Open field running drill.

Coaching Points: The ballcarrier must attempt all open-field running off a north-south run threat. Such an approach will help put the defender in somewhat of a bind while helping the ballcarrier to practice to always strive to gain positive yardage toward the end zone. All open-field running techniques, such as head and body faking, stutter stepping, limp-leg action, change of pace running, high stepping, cutting across the grain, drive blocking up the sideline, and spinning out, should be emphasized.

THE BACKFIELD OPTION GAME

The coaching of the backfield option game is certainly a broad topic. It is hard to discuss just one aspect, such as backfield play, without interrelating with some of the many other facets of offensive execution. It is, however, the purpose of this chapter to limit discussion to only quarterback and running back option execution. However, it will still be broad enough in scope so each coach can apply the information to his particular style of option play.

THE TRIPLE-OPTION DIVE READ

The triple-option dive read is the initial foundation of triple-option football, which refers to the quarterback's ability to execute a dive handoff, keep the ball himself, or pitch the ball to the pitchback, depending on the reactions of the defense. The reactions of the defense, or more specifically the isolated defenders, whether blocked or unblocked, are the key to option football. In the case of the triple option, three offensive threats—dive, deep, and pitch—attack two defenders, who can only properly react to two of the threats. By reading the defensive reactions, the quarterback determines which option to execute.

     The quarterback starts reading the initial dive key defender before the ball is snapped. Since the option game requires split second timing, the quarterback cannot wait until after the ball is snapped to locate the dive key defender. This individual is the defender who is designated as the player who must stop a particular dive threat. By scanning the defense as he addresses the center, the quarterback can usually determine who the dive key defender is, and often, how he is aligned. This information can help the quarterback anticipate which option might be appropriate. Anticipation is a major key to the success of the option play.

     The execution of the dive read takes on two design aspects: the dive read execution with a fullback, as in the "I" or Wishbone formations, and the dive read execution with a halfback, as in a split-back veer formation. The fullback dive-read relies on a mesh, ride-and-decide action, and the halfback dive-read relies more on a give or fake-give action.

     As mentioned in Chapter 3, the "I" or Wishbone fullback takes a fairly evenly balanced four-point stance, mainly because of the dive-read action. It is extremely important that the fullback's, or upback's, initial steps to the dive landmark are the same to both sides, to ensure a consistent mesh for the quarterback. The diveback's landmark can be anywhere from over the butt of the guard to the inside hip of the tackle, depending on the design of the offense.

The quarterback steps back on a 45-degree angle and delivers the ball on a direct line to the fullback's pouch. The quarterback does not swing the ball out with a straight arm action, but instead reaches back with the ball to create the desired straight arm action of the ride. He must use his peripheral vision to locate the ballcarrier's pouch, since he must be reading the dive key all through this action. The quarterback must make his read by the time the ball is ridden to his belt buckle. Continued riding of the ball past his belt buckle, toward his front leg, will only create a disturbance of timing and mesh, because the fullback's hip will begin to interfere with the coordination of the mesh, ride-and-decide sequence.

The read of the dive key is simple. If the dive key defender attacks the fullback by either closing down laterally in the hole or by taking a direct, penetrating angle charge at the fullback, the quarterback disconnects the ball from the fullback's pouch and options the keep-pitch key defender. If the dive key defender sits and reads, slants or loops to the outside, or penetrates straight ahead into the backfield, the ball is given to the fullback. This action is shown in Diagram 8-1 against a 5-2 defensive tackle dive key.

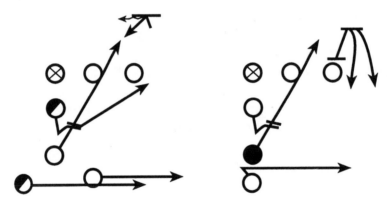

Diagram 8-1
Dive key read to the fullback.

Giving the ball to the fullback against a sitting dive key defender is generally thought to be the wiser decision. To pull the ball versus such a defender will often allow the dive key defender to react back to the quarterback, especially if he has made little commitment to the fullback. Whether the dive key defender is able to reach the quarterback or not, his reaction back to the quarterback will often be sufficient to disturb the play. A give to the fullback against a sitting dive key defender provides the safer option, since the fullback's "head of steam" should produce positive yardage against the more passive, sitting dive key defender. Whatever the philosophy, the decision to give the ball to the fullback will eventually force the dive key to "show his hand" earlier and make a more pronounced commitment one way or the other.

The emphasis in the dive read is on giving the ball to the fullback, unless the dive key defender reacts in a manner that dictates "pull." This emphasis helps create a firm ride of the ball in the fullback's pouch, a more precise handoff if the read dictates "give," and a better fake of the handoff if the read is "pull." The better fake is a result of the heavy sink of the ball into the fullback's pouch.

If the read is "give," the quarterback carries out his normal handoff technique. The ball, already on the handoff spot, is simply pressed up firmly against the fullback's pouch by the quarterback's outside hand as his inside hand is brought out from behind the ball. Remember, the inside hand is held just off the ball, to wait for the outside hand to come off the ball, so the two hands stay together to execute a proper fake of the keep-pitch option action. If the read is "pull," the quarterback disengages the ball from the fullback's pouch by snapping it forward away from the fullback's stomach, to facilitate pulling it out of the pouch, as he draws the ball to his sternum to carry out the keep-pitch portion of the option.

The quarterback's ride, or second step, is actually a feather type of action in which his front foot and leg are suspended in air as the ball is ridden forward toward the quarterback's belt buckle. If the read is "pull," the quarterback simply continues the midair suspension of the front foot and leg until the fullback passes him, and then redirects the foot down the line of scrimmage toward the keep-pitch key. Some coaches feel that the exact same action should be carried out if the read is "give" on the dive handoff. Other coaches feel that the front foot should follow the ride of the fullback and be planted on the ground to best accommodate the dive handoff. However, this action is executed at the expense of the keep-pitch fake action.

It is important to note that the dive handoff action, or the disengagement of the ball to carry out the keep-pitch option, should be as contrasting as possible. The ball must be either firmly handed off with a hard press of the ball against the fullback's pouch, or a heavy snapping action of the ball off the fullback's pouch must occur. There must be as little doubt as possible in the fullback's mind whether the action is give or pull. The fullback dive-mesh action is seen in Figure 8-1.

Initial mesh

Ride-and-decide action to the QB's belt buckle

**Figure 8-1
Quarterback-fullback dive-read execution.**

The halfback dive mesh is not able to utilize the fullback-type mesh action due to the distance the quarterback has to go to get to the mesh point and the angle of approach the halfback has to take to hit his landmark. A comparison of these mesh courses is shown in Diagram 8-2.

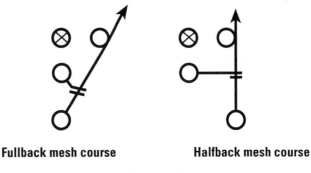

Fullback mesh course   **Halfback mesh course**

Diagram 8-2
Comparison of fullback and halfback dive-mesh courses.

The quarterback's initial two steps are straight down the line of scrimmage. His steps are controlled, which sets the quarterback in the area behind the guard (the exact positioning depends on the diveback's landmark). The quarterback attempts to make his dive-key read on his first to second step. The read may be carried all the way to the third adjustment-type step if a problem exists with the read.

The halfback dive-key read execution, therefore, is not "ride-and-decide." Instead, it is "give", or "fake-the-give." The read of the dive key is the same as it is for the fullback dive-key read execution (refer to Diagram 8-1). If the read is "give," the quarterback executes a normal dive handoff. The ball is firmly placed on the spot of the handoff pouch. The handoff must be made as deep as possible. The earlier the read, the greater the possibility of a deeper handoff. As on the ride-and-decide action with the fullback, the quarterback must use his peripheral vision to initially locate the halfback's handoff pouch. However, once the dive read is determined as "give," the quarterback must switch all concentration to the ballcarrier's handoff pouch.

The quarterback's third step is an adjustment-type step to help facilitate the mesh with the halfback. A tall, long-legged quarterback may actually not need a third or even a fourth step, since his first two steps might already position him properly for the mesh action. The fourth step takes on the same feather-type action of the fullback dive mesh, in which the front leg and foot are suspended during the give or fake action. Or, the front foot can step toward the line of scrimmage to help facilitate the give or fake to the halfback. This feather technique, whether for the dive fake or for the dive, lets the halfback pass by on his dive course until he clears the quarterback. At that time, the quarterback redirects his feather step down the line of scrimmage toward the keep-pitch key.

If the read is "keep," the quarterback fakes a dive handoff by reaching back with the ball to place it on the forward hip of the halfback (compared to the on-the-belly if "give") and rides the diveback to his belt buckle. Due to the timing of the mesh, this faking action may be little more than a jabbing, waving action. The quarterback must be sure, however, to execute this faking action in order to delay his down-the-line action long enough to allow the pitchback to move into his proper pitch ratio. A quarterback who breaks out of the mesh too quickly breaks down the timing needed to allow for proper positioning of the pitchbacks in the option design.

THE OUTSIDE VEER TRIPLE-OPTION DIVE READ

Execution of the outside veer triple option dive read is similar to that of the half-back dive mesh. The only major difference is that in the outside veer dive, the mesh point is one hole farther down the line of scrimmage. The quarterback positions himself approximately behind the tackle. His stepping is a four-step action. However, his third step is not an adjustment step, but rather a healthy full step to get him to the widened dive mesh point. This third step, however, is slightly back toward the diveback, as on the third step of the normal inside veer mesh. The quarterback then carries out the "give" or "fake-give" dive-key read execution.

THE COUNTER-OPTION TRIPLE-OPTION DIVE READ

Although not very common, some teams utilize triple-option action on the counter option, instead of predetermining the dive and option actions. The counter-option triple-option action takes on the mechanics of the fullback dive-mesh execution on the inside veer. The quarterback, on his four-step reverse pivot action, steps back deeply on his third step to place the ball in the diveback's pouch, then snaps his head to the dive key. The normal ride-and-decide action is carried out as the fourth, adjustment-type slide step is brought up to the third step to accommodate either the dive-give or the dive-fake action. The fifth step is then taken with the back foot—the same foot as the fourth, adjustment-type step—as it is redirected on a 30-degree angle downhill attack course, to option the keep-pitch key defender.

THE KEEP-PITCH READ DOWNHILL ATTACK

Essential to the attack of the keep-pitch key is a hard, downhill attack, meaning that the quarterback takes an approximate 30-degree angle toward the line of scrimmage. This angle of attack is taken either immediately–lead option–or after some type of dive fake–inside veer, counter option, or trap option (refer to Diagram 8-3). The downhill attack is not executed, however, on the outside veer option.

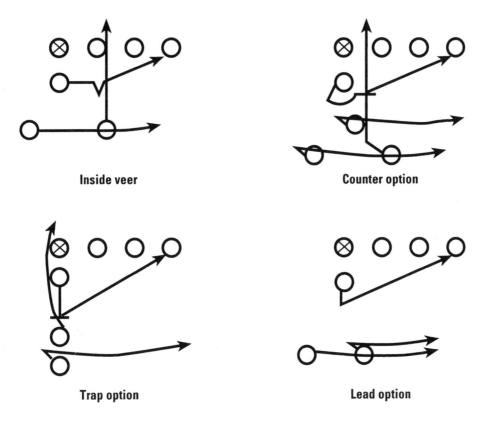

Diagram 8-3
Keep-pitch key read downhill attack.

The concept behind the downhill attack is that it puts pressure on the keep-pitch defender, forces him to make a more pronounced commitment sooner, and allows the option action a shorter corner to turn to gain north-south yardage.

Attacking downhill on a 30-degree angle puts the keep-pitch key defender in a bind or "sweat." The upfield, positive-yardage angle of the quarterback's attack forces the keep-pitch key defender to take a pronounced, sharper angle of attack to get to the quarterback–similar to a closing-down type of action on an off-tackle play–if he is the defender assigned to the quarterback. This action is shown in Diagram 8-4, from lead-option action.

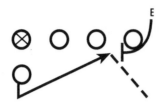

Diagram 8-4
Downhill attack forcing a sharp angle of attack by
the keep-pitch key dictating a pitch.

Forcing the keep-pitch defender into such a pronounced, sharper attack angle enables a sharper corner for the pitchback to turn in his drive to gain straight-ahead yardage. This action is shown in Diagram 8-5, in which a downhill attack is compared with a flatter, down-the-line attack that creates a more rounded course for the pitchback, delaying his north-south progress.

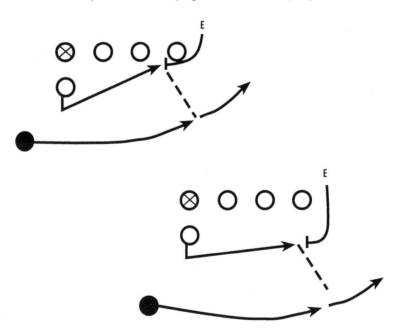

Diagram 8-5
Comparison of the effect of a downhill attack to a non-downhill attack.

The differences of the pitchback routes shown in Diagram 8-4 are extremely significant. If the pitchback is able to turn up sharply as a result of the quarterback's downhill attack and move north-south more quickly, he will create a greater opportunity to beat the pursuit of the interior defenders. As on any corner running action, the more a ballcarrier has to run east-west, or sideways, to turn the corner, the more chance the defenders have of being able to pursue and run him down before he can turn the corner and get upfield for a maximum north-south yardage gain.

Once the deep-pitch defender commits to the quarterback, which means he is positioned so he can no longer get to the pitchback, the quarterback attempts to flatten out at the keep-pitch key defender's downfield shoulder, so that the defender is shielded away from and unable to interfere with the pitching action. This movement would be in contrast to a continued line of attack that would position the quarterback directly in front of the keep-pitch key defender, or even worse, inside of him. A position by the quarterback directly in front of the defender will enable the defender to interfere with the pitch, since the pitch will have to go through him. Examples of this situation are shown in Diagram 8-6— again using the lead option for illustration.

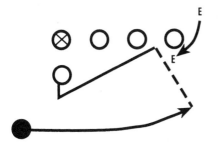

Inside attack, giving defender an excellent chance to interfere with the pitch

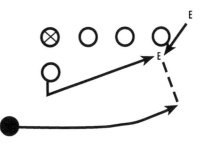

Attacking directly at defender, giving a good chance to interfere with the pitch

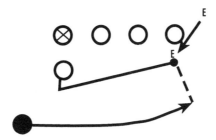

Flattening out to downfield shoulder, eliminating defender's ability to interfere with the pitch

Diagram 8-6
Flattened-out and non-flattened-out attack against the keep-pitch defender.

The optimal situation for the quarterback is to attack the keep-pitch key defender's downfield shoulder by flattening out his course, stepping out toward the pitchback, and looking directly to the pitch spot. It must be understood, however, that sometimes it may not be possible for the quarterback to flatten out his course and attack the defender's downfield shoulder. Varied attacks and styles of play by the defender and two-defender cross-charge actions will force less-than-optimal pitch actions, such as coming out of a dive fake early in order to execute an immediate pitch, pitching in the midst of taking a step, pitching off an inside-foot step, etc.

A crash-type charge by the keep-pitch key defender is the most drastic action the quarterback must deal with, especially when the quarterback is executing a dive fake or is coming out of a triple-option read pull action. In this regard, two points are important. Initially, the quarterback must disengage from the fake action immediately upon the read of the crash charge in order to initiate the pitch action. Again, a commitment by the keep-pitch defender occurs when he is in a position where he can no longer react to the pitchback. A crash charge usually puts the defender in this position immediately. It also eliminates his ability to interfere with the pitch. Secondly, the quarterback must be sure to bring the ball back to his sternum before pitching, to allow for the proper pitching action as discussed in Chapter 7.

Another problem that the quarterback must be concerned with regarding the defender's heavy crash-type charge is how to absorb the blow of contact with the defender after the pitch has been executed. The quarterback should simply give with the blow as much as possible to minimize the hard contact.

Perhaps the most difficult keep-pitch defender's technique for the quarterback to deal with is the lightly feathering defender who is playing the "cat and mouse" technique well. Such a defender shows neither a commitment to the pitch nor to the keep action. The worst mistake the quarterback can make in this situation, and the most common, is to slow down his attack and/or to flatten out his downhill attack at the defender more parallel to the line of scrimmage before the defender has committed to the quarterback. This action only helps give the interior defenders time to pursue the play as the quarterback directs the option action on the undesirable east-west course. This plays right into the hands of the lightly feathering defender, helping to string out the play to the sideline. This undesired action is illustrated in Diagram 8-7, using a lead option play as an example.

Diagram 8-7
Undesired slow down and/or flattening out action of the QB
vs. a lightly feathering keep-pitch key defender.

The desirable way for the quarterback to handle the lightly feathering deep-pitch key defender is in the same manner he would in any other situation. He must attack on his 30-degree downhill course at top speed in order to force the defender to react and commit one way or the other. If the defender continues to feather, the quarterback will suddenly realize that he is even with, or beyond the defender, thus dictating the keep option. If the defender slows down to react to the quarterback, the quarterback will flatten out his course to the defender's downhill shoulder and execute the pitch.

If the keep-pitch key defender feathers heavily (flies out laterally), penetrates across the line of scrimmage, or loops to the outside to take on a pitch-support action, the quarterback's 30-degree downhill attack will help the quarterback's decision making process by dictating "keep," according to the relationship of the quarterback to the defender. By staying on his course, the quarterback will see that he will eventually become even with or go past the keep-pitch key defender, which tells the quarterback to plant his outside foot and head upfield. This action is shown in Diagram 8-8.

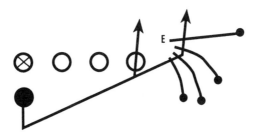

Diagram 8-8
Downhill attack dictating QB keep due to the keep-pitch key feather or
penetration action by the defender.

Two important points about these keep-read actions need to be examined. Initially, the quarterback must scan upfield as he cuts north-south, to be sure that some sort of cross charge isn't taking place. If a cross charge is occurring, he then simply carries out his normal pitch action, attacking the new keep-pitch key defender's downfield shoulder (refer to Diagram 8-9).

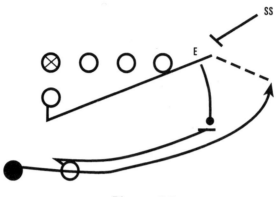

Diagram 8-9
Optioning cross-charge action.

Secondly, when the quarterback plants his outside foot in order to head upfield, his initial aiming point is upfield toward the end zone flag. This emphasis enables north-south yardage while getting away from the inside pursuit. A sharper north-south cut might put the quarterback into the thick of this inside-out pursuit. Of course, running to daylight always takes precedence.

On all downhill attacking of the deep-pitch key defender, it is important that the quarterback think "pitch" first and "keep" second. The pitchback is the priority player to carry the ball, just as the diveback was on the dive-keep option. The main purpose of the keep-pitch option is to execute the downhill attack to force the keep-pitch key defender to commit to the quarterback, so that the pitch can be accomplished. A keep by the quarterback is simply a reaction to the play of the keep-pitch key defender, and is actually the quarterback's last choice.

INSIDE VEER OPTION ACTION

The inside veer dive action, whether to a halfback or a fullback, has already been discussed in this chapter. The only point that needs further mentioning is the quarterback's initial redirection step down the line of scrimmage. If his fourth step in the dive-mesh action is a feather step, the quarterback simply hangs the inside leg and foot in the air long enough for the diveback to pass him, then whips this inside foot out on the desired 30-degree angle downhill attack path.

If the fourth step is a plant step toward the line of scrimmage to facilitate the dive action, then the back foot initiates the 30-degree angle downhill attack course. In both cases, as soon as the quarterback begins to pull the ball from the dive-fake action, he must immediately switch his eyes to the keep-pitch key defender, to pick up any possible crash charge. In addition, he must immediately pull the ball up to his sternum to be ready for immediate pitch situations.

LEAD OPTION ACTION

The quarterback's initial action to get into the desired 30-degree angle downhill attack course is a three-step action, with the first two steps moving him back from the center to help create the downhill angle (refer to Diagram 8-10). In addition, the first two delay-type steps help to freeze the linebackers while giving the pitchback time to get into a proper pitch relationship.

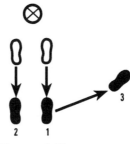

Diagram 8-10
Lead option QB steps.

The quarterback's first two steps are straight back, the first step taken with the foot to the side of the option action. The second step, with the foot away from the option side, is a plant-type step, from which he pivots and pushes off to take his 30-degree downhill third step with the foot to the option side. The second step is slightly deeper than the first. These first two steps must not reveal any direction that the option will be run via the quarterback's turning his body toward the option side. The intent of this action is to attempt to freeze the linebackers in position by not revealing any direction cues until the third step.

COUNTER-OPTION ACTION

The quarterback's counter-option stepping action was already discussed in both Chapter 4 and this chapter. It should be further emphasized, however, that on his third redirection step back toward the counter diveback, the quarterback must snap his head to see the keep-pitch key defender to read any possible crash-type charge by the defender. If the play calls for triple-option counter-option action, this action would, of course, take place after the dive read. The fifth redirection step in the 30-degree downhill angle attack course, with the back foot, after the counter dive fake, is again a key coaching point. No bellying action off the desired downhill course should occur. It must be a sharp, 30-degree angle downhill attack step. As on all other option actions, the quarterback must be sure to bring the ball to his sternum as soon as he comes out of his counter-dive action stepping.

TRAP-OPTION ACTION

The quarterback's initial action to get onto the desired 30-degree downhill attack course is a three-step action with the first step facilitating the dive fake. The first step is taken with the foot away from the option action (refer to Diagram 8-11).

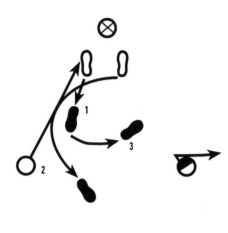
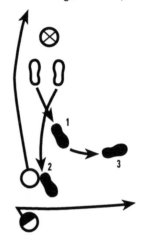

Split backfield trap-option steps   **"I" formation trap-option steps**

Diagram 8-11
Trap-option QB steps.

It is a deep, 135-degree-plus step if the fake is to a halfback, and a 180-degree-plus step if the fake is to a fullback. The ball is extended out toward the diveback's pouch, but is never placed in the pouch. The second step is a crossover step that continues on the same plane as the first step. However, it goes beyond the first step by about 18 inches. Actually, this plant step turns the toes slightly in the direction of the crossover to facilitate pushing off for the third step—the 30-degree downhill step.

It is important for the quarterback to snap his head around fast as the second step is planted, to enable him to see the keep-pitch key defender and read his possible crash charge. Also, he must immediately bring the ball back to his sternum on the second step to help facilitate a possible immediate pitch action. Diagram 8-11 shows this action from both split-back and "I" formation alignments.

OUTSIDE VEER OPTION ACTION

The outside veer option action takes on a different execution technique, due to the wider mesh with the diveback, since his landmark is one hole wider and involves a different attack angle by the keep-pitch key defender. It must be remembered that the outside veer double-team blocks the normal dive key and forces the normal keep-pitch key to become the dive key, thereby forcing the normal contain defender to become the keep-pitch key. This action is shown in Diagram 8-12 from a split-back alignment. The design of the play is actually premised on forcing defenders to take on option assignments that they are not used to executing.

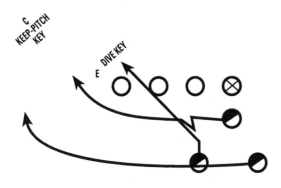

Diagram 8-12
Outside veer keys.

Due to the wider mesh point with the diveback, most quarterbacks find it quite difficult to utilize the feather technique with the inside foot on the fourth step. Another reason it is difficult to use the feather-type fourth step is that the quarterback's keep-pitch key attack action is not the typical 30-degree downhill attack. Instead, it is a bouncing type action in an effort to jump around the collision of the diveback and the dive key defender and to attack upfield at the keep-pitch key defender.

The fourth step, therefore, is a slight adjustment step into the line of scrimmage to accommodate the dive-mesh action (refer to Diagram 8-13). The fifth step is a "jump-around" type step around the collision point of the diveback and the dive key defender. The important point about performing this step properly is that the quarterback tries to keep his foot no closer than parallel to the line of scrimmage to preserve a good north-south push off for attacking the keep-pitch key defender. The key to this entire action is to get around the collision of the diveback and the dive key defender as quickly and as tightly as possible. The farther from the line of scrimmage the quarterback steps, the slower will be his north-south attack, thereby giving the interior defenders a better chance to pursue. Once the quarterback bounces around the collision point, he attacks north-south and options the keep-pitch key defender just as he would option a perimeter-type defender who is attacking on a cross-charge type action against an inside veer keep-pitch action by the quarterback.

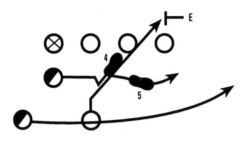

Diagram 8-13
Outside veer QB keep steps.

QUARTERBACK-PITCHBACK PITCH RATIO

The quarterback-pitchback pitch ratio is always the pitchback's responsibility. Whatever the ratio might be (3-1/2 by 3-1/2 yards, 4 by 4 yards, etc.), the pitchback must be sure that his distance and angle from the quarterback are identical for all option plays. The timings may differ, but the distance and angle between them must be consistent.

The pitchback must realize that no matter what the quarterback does, or is forced to do, the pitchback must maintain the pitch ratio. If the quarterback slows down, is forced to bounce around a block, elongates his attack on a feathering keep-pitch key defender, or bounces off a collision of blockers and defenders, the pitchback must always be in the exact spot of the desired pitch ratio. Even if the quarterback's action is incorrect, the pitchback must maintain the correct pitch ratio, so that a good pitch can be executed.

Once the quarterback cuts upfield, the pitchback must continue to trail the quarterback wherever he goes, to be ready for a possible pitch further upfield. In this case, however, the ratio changes. The same width distance is maintained, but the pitchback trails the quarterback by a yard to a yard-and-a-half. This situation is shown in Diagram 8-14 from inside veer option action.

An important point for all keep-pitch key option action is that the quarter-back must come out of the dive fake if there is one, and accelerate at top speed. A major fault of many quarterbacks is a slow acceleration, either out of the dive fake, or just down the line of scrimmage, as on lead option action. A slow acceleration merely gives time for the defense to pursue the option action and give support to defending both the keep and pitch possibilities.

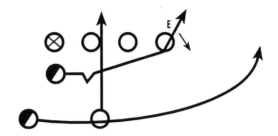

Diagram 8-14
Upfield pitch ratio.

BACKFIELD OPTION PRACTICE AND DRILLS

Only one correct way exists for practicing option skills—set up a game-like enactment of an option play, or as part of an option play, against various defenses and their various styles of defending options. Other than practicing pure pitch skill work and reception skills, only such game-like drill work truly helps to develop the skills necessary to execute the option game on the field. Because several pure pitch drills were already shown in Chapter 7, only one such drill will be included in this chapter, along with several option-pitch drills.

Drill #1: Down-the-Line Pitch

The down-the-line pitch drill is a pure quarterback pitch-skill drill which helps develop proper pitching action. Two quarterbacks work down two 5-yard lines, as shown in Diagram 8-15, with their distance apart modified to coincide with the desired pitch ratio. One quarterback holds the ball on his sternum, ready to pitch the ball, and jogs in place. The other runs out away from him down his own yard line to create the proper pitch-option ratio. Once the proper ratio is established, the quarterback with the ball takes off down his line and executes his normal pitch action to the other quarterback out in front of him. When the other quarterback receives the pitch, he jogs in place until the first one has run ahead to the proper pitch ratio, at which time he takes off down his line and executes his normal pitch to the quarterback out in front of him. They repeat this action, leap-frog style, all the way across the field.

Coaching Points: The quarterbacks must be sure to turn around and come back the way they came, so that they practice pitching the ball to both sides.

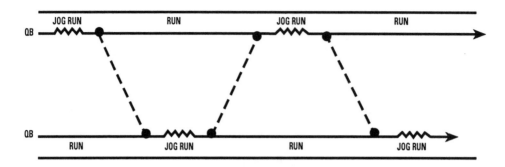

Diagram 8-15
Down-the-line pitch drill.

Drill #2: Rapid-Fire Option Pitch

This drill allows for maximum practice of pitch-keep key reads, reactions, and option pitches. Two quarterbacks work back and forth on a line of scrimmage tape, versus a simulated defensive end, and carry out normal option actions (refer to Diagram 8-16). After each repetition, the quarterbacks switch roles as quarterback and pitchback. After two repetitions, the quarterbacks retrace their first two repetitions in order to practice the option from both their left and right sides.

Coaching Points: The player simulating the defensive end varies his defensive option play on each repetition. He can sit, penetrate, crash, feather lightly, feather heavily, etc. The coach can jump in occasionally, or a second defender may be used, to create cross-charge situations. Thus, the coach is checking all the proper quarterback reactions to the defensive play—"keep" or "pitch"—plus proper pitching actions.

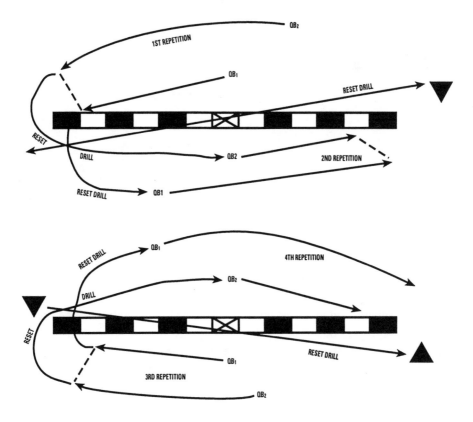

Diagram 8-16
Rapid fire option-pitch drill.

Drill #3: Dive Read

The dive read drill is an isolated segment of triple-option action to practice the dive read portion. It can be run anywhere from live-action to a third type of action using hand bags or shields. The defender is given signals indicating what type of defensive pattern to run and how to react. Diagram 8-17 shows the dive read drill, practicing an inside veer dive read to a Wishbone or "I' formation fullback and an outside veer dive read to a split-back formation halfback.

Coaching Points: The coach must be sure to vary the actions of the defender. All mesh skills, landmark running, reading action, handoff skills, acceleration from the mesh by the quarterback, faking action, etc., should be checked by the coach. The coach must be sure to work the reading action to both sides.

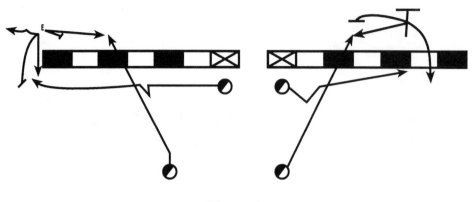

Diagram 8-17
The dive read drill.

Drill #4: Triple-Option Read

The triple-option read drill carries the dive read drill one step further. A second and third defender are added to the drill. The quarterback and other backs now carry out their normal triple-option action against the defensive alignment and reactions specified. For example, Diagram 8-18 illustrates the inside veer triple-option action from a split backfield set.

Coaching Points: The coach must be sure to vary the defensive alignments and reactions. The third defender can be utilized to add occasional cross-charge actions. The coach must again be sure to work both sides.

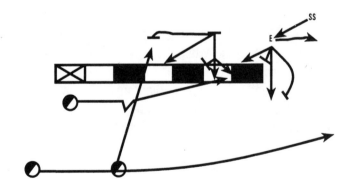

Diagram 8-18
The triple-option drill.

Drill #5: Individual Option

The individual option drill is identical to the triple-option drill, except that it practices option plays that only have a double option potential—lead option, counter option, trap option, or predetermined inside veer option and outside veer option. Thus, a dive key defender is not used, since the quarterback is only optioning a keep-pitch key defender and a possible linebacker or strong safety/ cornerback on some type of cross-charge action. Diagram 8-19 shows the drill with trap-option action as an example.

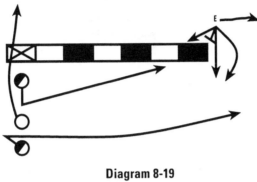

Diagram 8-19
The individual option drill.

Drill #6: Multiple-Option

The multiple-option drill is an excellent option drill that helps achieve maximum repetitions of the option actions. It actually combines all the actions of the dive read, triple option, and individual option drills into one game-like drill. As in the other drills, it can be simply executed against defenders using non-contact action (perhaps using hand bags or shields), or it can be run live, or semi-live. Two tapes or hoses are laid out with the center's "X"s on the hash marks (refer to Diagram 8-20). A skeleton defense is set up utilizing those defenders needed to make all the necessary reads. Two offensive backfields are used to get maximum repetitions and to avoid wasting time. The first repetition is started on the left tape and is an option play run toward the left sideline. The coach checks all the desired backfield option skills. As the first backfield finishes the play's execution, the second backfield is ready, and repeats the same play. As the second backfield finishes its execution of the drill, the first backfield is set up to execute an option play to the right—into the open field. When they finish, they set up on the tape on the right hash mark, as the second backfield repeats the same play. When the second backfield finishes, they hustle behind the first backfield as the first backfield gets ready to start the whole process over again. After the first four repetitions from the left hash mark, the defenders switch to the tape on the right hash mark. Thus,

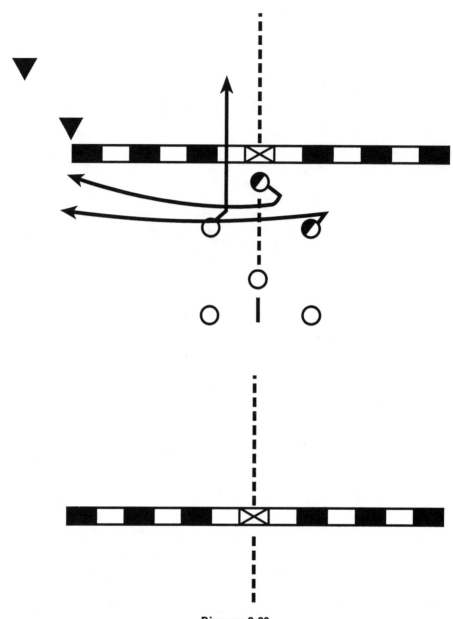

Diagram 8-20
The multiple-option drill in its simplest form.

four option plays are run from the left hash mark—two toward the sideline and two to the wide side of the field—and four plays are run from the right hash mark—two to the sideline and two to the wide side. The plays are run in rapid-fire action to ensure maximum repetitions—one backfield beginning as soon as the other finishes. The drill may be set up simply, practicing only running double option plays against two service defenders, as shown in Diagram 8-21, in which the defense uses all of their players who are involved in the optioning action, as the offense adds its tight end to stalk-block or to seal inside linebackers.

Coaching Points: It is important to note that if a defender is not blocked by the skeleton offensive unit, he does not interfere with the execution of the option action. In the multiple-option drill, it is good to have a second coach to help expedite the action of the defense. In addition, the drill must also be practiced with the tapes placed halfway between the hash marks and the center of the field, as well as in the center of the field, to simulate all actual game-ball placements. Thus, the important dimensions of lateral space, sidelines, and field bevelment, (i.e., the crown) are included in the drill. Concern for field bevelment or crown, is an aspect of option play preparation that is often grossly overlooked. A pitchback will definitely run faster downhill toward the sideline, just as he will run significantly slower uphill toward the center crown of the field. This variable must be taken into account because of the necessity of split second timing and exact quarterback-pitchback ratios on all option plays. This factor, of course, does not apply to a flat, non-beveled, or non-crowned field.

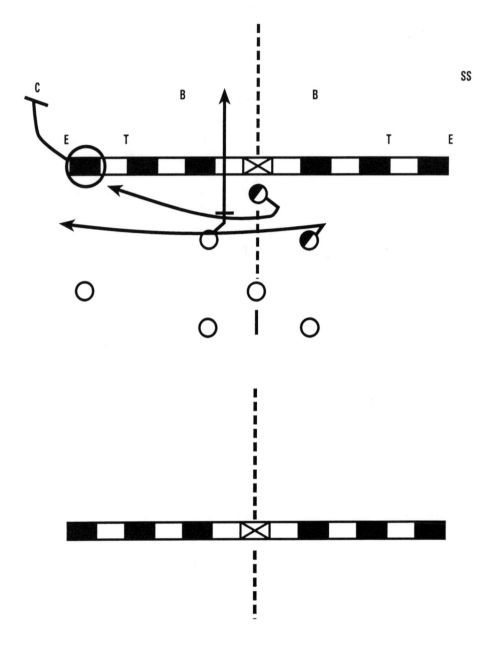

Diagram 8-21
The multiple-option drill in its most complex form utilizing
tight ends vs. a skeleton defense.

Drill #7: Perimeter Option

The perimeter option drill simply combines the backfield option action with the receiver blocking actions. It helps players practice the timing of the backfield option action with the perimeter blocks and helps coordinate possible switching of blocking assignments of lead backs and wide receivers, or inside receivers, in situations such as on cross-blocking assignments. All of the option plays used in the offense are practiced to both sides. Enough defenders are used to help create all of the necessary option reads, as well as to provide perimeter defenders for the perimeter blocking actions. This drill is shown in Diagram 8-22, using a lead-option play with a cross-blocking scheme as an example.

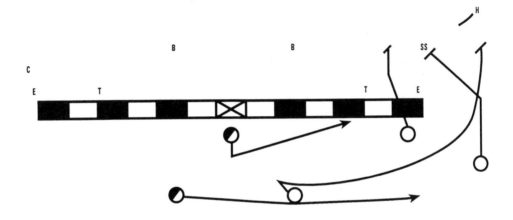

Diagram 8-22
The perimeter option drill.

133

CHAPTER 9

QUARTERBACK PASS TECHNIQUES

Just as with a truly great runner, the naturally great passer is more the exception than the rule. More often than not, the coach must teach and develop skills and techniques that are not inherent in his passing quarterback. Since much of passing relies on technique, however, the requisite attributes can be taught and developed.

Far too often, a team doesn't pass because it doesn't have a good passer. Also far too often, the team doesn't have a good passer because he hasn't been coached properly. Fortunately, sound passing techniques can be taught, coached, practiced, and drilled.

It is extremely important to remember when coaching a passer that no two individuals throw in exactly the same manner. Thus, the coach should not try to impose strict fundamental rules on how to pass. Instead, he should help the individual quarterback to perform to the best of his ability. Biomechanical differences should be analyzed and addressed to help each passer get the most out of his particular style. Just as there is a great variety of pitching styles among successful baseball pitchers, a similar variety of passing styles also exist for quarterbacks.

GRIPPING THE FOOTBALL

The quarterback should assume a firm, comfortable grip in which the ball is gripped by the fingers, the thumb, and the heel of his hand. It should not be palmed, because palming, along with placing the index finger too far from the end of the ball, causes a hard, nose-down, sinking flight of the ball, which is relatively difficult to catch. Instead, daylight should exist between the palm and the ball, and the passer's index finger should be extended toward the rear of the ball. This action helps to get the nose of the ball up, which in turn produces a softer, easier-to-catch pass.

The specific grip of the football may vary—with a small-handed quarterback gripping more toward the end and a larger-handed passer gripping more toward the middle. Wherever the ball is gripped, however, the fingers must be well spread, in order to enhance the quarterback's control of the ball and help produce a spiral-type pass. Generally, the last three fingers of the quarterback's passing hand are placed across the laces as the index finger extends toward the end of the ball, with the thumb naturally wrapped around in the opposite direction to produce a firm, comfortable grip (refer to Figure 9-1).

Figure 9-1
Proper grip of the ball for passing.

SETTING UP

Setting up requires movement of the launch point, stopping and assuming the cocked position, so that a quick release delivery can be executed. The launch point is back away from the line of scrimmage, and usually inside the tackle-to-tackle area from which the quarterback will launch (or throw) his pass from a fixed,(or "set") position, while remaining stationary (i.e., not moving). Throwing on the move (e.g., a sprint pass) will be discussed separately.

Drop-back movement to a set position can take the form of a straight drop-back pedal, sprint back, a combination of the two, or it can be a quarter roll, half roll, throw back, or some type of play-action set up. Since such a wide variety of drop-back set up actions exist, and since these can vary greatly depending on the philosophy of the set up action (e.g., selling sprint-action influence to set up the throwback pass, dump-passing to hot receivers, etc.), only the key points of the drop-back movement to the launch point will be discussed. These factors are depth and speed of the drop-back action, throttling down and stopping, and assuming the cocked throwing position.

Depth and speed of getting to the launch point are extremely important, whether the drop-back action is a seven-step, straight drop-back set up to throw to a curl pattern, or it's a fake isolation play-action pass. Actually, depth of the set up and speed in getting to the launch point go hand in hand. The faster a quarterback can set up at his launch point, the less protection he will need from his blockers, since this action allows him more time to read the defense and/or receivers and to get the pass off. The same concept relates to the depth of set up in a given number of steps. For example, if on a five-step, straight drop-back pocket set-up, one quarterback is a yard-and-a-half deeper than another in the same number of steps, he will not need as much protection as the other. As a result, he will have more time to read both defense and receivers.

Vision is a major key on all set up actions. Viewing the defense will enable the quarterback either to unload the ball if he is faced with an overloaded blitz from the linebackers or secondary defenders or to move away from rushers if his protection breaks down. Certain types of drop-back set ups offer the quarterback greater vision than others. However, no matter which set up technique is used, vision is enhanced by a quick and deep set up that gives the quarterback more time for looking at the situation.

Whatever drop-back action is utilized for the set up, the first one, three, or five steps of the drop-back are premised on getting maximum depth behind the line of scrimmage. Depth of step, turning the toes away from the line of scrimmage, and body lean affect the depth of drop. The quarterback also must be sure to smoothly rock the cradled ball in front of his chest as he drops back. This action helps to expedite his drop-back action more than if he holds the ball in an already cocked-to-throw position.

In all drop-back actions, the last two steps involve the same techniques. The next to last step is a throttle-down step, and the last step is a plant or stop step. The throttle-down step shifts much of the backward momentum of the body's weight back toward the line of scrimmage. This throttle-down action helps bring the body's momentum under enough control so that the last step can act as a brake to stop the backward movement for the set up. This final plant, or stop step, can put the quarterback in the cocked position, ready to deliver the pass. The majority of his body weight is on his back foot, ready to be transferred to his front foot during the launch or delivery action. Both knees are slightly bent, also to accommodate the delivery movement. Placing the weight on the balls of the feet, not the heels, also facilitates delivery, as well as balance in the cocked position. Figure 9-2 illustrates the proper technique of bent knees, body lean, throttle-down, and plant. However, on most throw actions, the quarterback will need to step up quickly with two short "settle" steps to enable him to gather his feet properly to enact the desired throw.

Figure 9-2
The QB in position to throw the ball.

The ball should be held in a gathered position in front of the chest, nearest the throwing arm, so that the ball has a minimum distance to go backwards for the delivery motion. The term "gathered," in this sense, refers to the gathering in of all the body parts in preparation for the action of transferring the body weight from the back to the front foot and directing the body's momentum into the delivery of the ball. The ball should not, however, be held so closely to the body that it restricts the delivery motion of the arm in any way. The free hand is placed on the ball during the set up action to help provide ball security in case the quarterback is blind-side tackled. The back, or throwing arm, shoulder in the set up must be cocked. In other words, it should not need to go any farther backward before executing delivery of the ball. The back elbow should be up and away from the body to help produce a level carry of both shoulders. If the back elbow is tucked in tight to the body, this action tends to shift the passer's weight to his back foot, causing a weak or off-balance throw. Figure 9-3 illustrates these set up points.

Figure 9-3
In setting up, the QB's back shoulder must be cocked.

THE DELIVERY OF THE BALL—THE THROW

Proper delivery of the ball, or a sound throwing technique, can greatly improve the passing of even quarterbacks who have been deemed weak-armed. Many times, a quarterback has a problem which is mostly due to his weight not transfering from his back to his front foot. Proper weight transfer helps put body momentum and thrust behind the action of the arm. Many quarterbacks sit back on their feet and "wing" the ball with a whipping action of the arm alone. This movement produces a passing action that is like "throwing a grenade"—too much trajectory and too little power.

The concept of weight transfer is best seen in the action of a baseball pitcher. When he winds up, all of his weight is on his back foot, and his front leg is kicked up and out in front. It is then swung forward and down toward the delivery spot, helping to propel his front hip forward. All of this action helps whip his upper torso—trunk, chest, shoulder, and then arm—toward the delivery spot. The transfer of his weight from his back foot to his front foot adds thrust to the delivery of the ball. Throwing a football follows these same basic principles. Proper and improper weight transfer are shown in Figure 9-4.

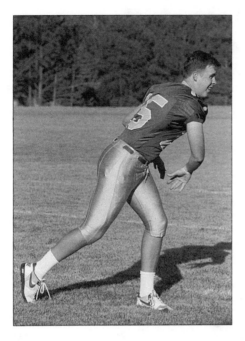

Figure 9-4
Proper (left photo) and improper (right photo) weight transfer.

From a fairly tight or bunched positioning of his feet to help eliminate over-striding, the quarterback pushes off the back foot as he steps toward the intended delivery spot. The target is not necessarily the receiver, but usually the point where the flight of the ball will intersect the receiver's route. The passer must actually attempt to point his toes at the delivery spot to help direct the total body motion to that spot. As the forward stepping takes place, the hips swing around on the same plane and help to whip the upper torso, and eventually the arm action, in the same direction. The balance of the body is actually regained from the transfer of weight from the back to the front foot, once the front foot is planted on the ground. The action of the hips—degree of opening toward the target spot—actually affects the forward step. Pointing the toes beyond the target spot could be the result of over-opening the hips and could cause the ball to be overthrown beyond the receiver. Pointing the toes behind the target spot may be the result of under-opening the hips and will likely cause the ball to be thrown behind the receiver.

The arm's throwing action is similar to the motion of a baseball catcher's peg to second base or the throwing of darts. The optimal throw is a direct over-hand throw. However, most quarterbacks find that they are more comfortable with a throwing plane substantially less than directly overhead. Again, individual style must be accommodated to help each passer produce his own most efficient throwing technique. Whatever the angle, the ball must be released as high as

140

possible to allow the fullest possible range of motion of the arm, as well as enabling the pass to clear the raised hands of the pass rushers.

The throwing action of the arm is actually one continuous, coordinated two-part motion. The ball is cocked in the approximate area off the back shoulder, yet still is slightly out in front of the front of the body. The elbow is drawn back so that the upper arm is approximately parallel to the ground. The bend or the extension of the arm in the cocked position depends on what is comfortable to the individual. The position of the ball, the position of the upper arm relative to the ground, and the bend or extension of the elbow can be described only in approximate terms, due to the variations that occur to accommodate the various distances and trajectories the ball must be thrown. In the cocked position, the elbow is slightly in front of the ball.

The forward motion of the ball delivery begins with the free hand and arm. The free hand and arm are extended outward toward the target spot to start the motion of leading with the chest. In an attempt to actually drive the ball with the chest, sticking out or leading with the chest helps put maximum upper torso thrust into the delivery. Of course, all of this upper body action is really a continuous complex movement, coordinated with the stepping-out and hip whipping actions.

It is important that the wrist be kept firm and straight during the delivery to help avoid a wobbly pass. The wrist should never be turned in an attempt to produce a spin on the ball. The natural action of a straight wrist delivery will help produce the desired spiral spin. The actual release of the ball is a screwball delivery action in which the thumb is pronated down toward the ground so that the palm is facing downward also. The ball is snapped off with a snapping action of the wrist and a full extension or lock of the elbow to help put extra snap or zip into the release. The ball should leave the index finger last, not the ring finger.

The motion to the cocked position and the action of the forward release of the ball are, again, executed in one continuous motion as if throwing a dart, but in a more circular manner. Speed of delivery for the desired quick release is not just dependent on the quarterback's ability to move the ball forward from the cocked position to the release. Far more often, a slow release results from using a wind-up motion to the cocked position. Other common actions that can contribute to a slow release are holding the ball too low, holding the ball too close to the body or to the midline of the body instead of in front of the chest, and not having the back shoulder fully cocked, thereby requiring further movement in drawing the shoulder backward. All of these actions can slow down the delivery of the ball.

FOLLOW-THROUGH

Another key to effective passing is proper follow-through. The most common error in passing is lack of proper follow-through. Pointing with the index finger of the throwing hand as the ball is released is the most important factor of follow-through. A good coaching point is that where the index finger points as the ball is released is where the ball will go. Of course, many other factors contribute to success, but proper follow-through greatly increases the chance of successful passing. The hand and index finger are, however, not suspended in air, pointing. The index finger points only for a fleeting moment at the release of the ball, then the hand and arm continue to follow through across the body and down toward the ground as the hand is pronated—thumb and palm down.

Another key factor is full extension, or lock, of the elbow, which helps to produce the full range of arm movement. Commonly, when a quarterback needs to throw a soft pass, he will release the ball before the arm reaches full extension, with his hand frozen at the release point rather than naturally following through. However, in this case, as on any pass, full follow-through must be executed. Softness, or "touch," can be accomplished by taking force out of the upper body and arm thrust. Proper arm and hand follow-through must be performed in order to ensure the proper flight of the ball.

PASSING TRAJECTORY

Varying the distance of a pass is less difficult than varying the trajectory. Many quarterbacks can hit targets all over the field with direct-line passes, but ask them to hit the same targets with greater loft on the ball, and they are lost. Passing to the same point with varied trajectories is difficult. However, with proper coaching and practice plus attention on executing proper techniques, greater ease and reliability can be developed in achieving a particular trajectory on a thrown ball.

Getting greater loft into the trajectory of a pass is simply a matter of adjusting the horizontal plane of the shoulders by adjusting the front arm and hand and the rear passing arm. The greater the height and/or distance of the desired pass, the greater the tilt will be of the horizontal shoulder plane. The front shoulder elevates the front arm on the free hand and arm reach out higher as they are extended to start the throwing motion. At the same time, the rear throwing shoulder drops, as well as the throwing elbow. As a result, the throwing hand and ball are cocked. The ultimate key, however, is the throwing elbow, since its position directly correlates to the forward throwing motion of the ball. The release will be higher and earlier. As a result, the wrist action will involve a slightly straight wrist release. Index finger pointing, thumb-down pronation of the hand, and proper follow-through of the throwing hand and arm are still carried out.

The greatest problem passers have in "touch" or trajectory passing is throwing a nose-up, floating ball that hangs in the air at its zenith, then dies, losing its forward thrust and falling quickly, still nose up. This type of floater will often throw the receiver off and fall short, underthrown. The key to preventing this type of floater is, again, proper follow-through–making sure that the index finger is pointing at a fixed point in the air that the ball must pass through at its zenith to get the desired trajectory. In addition, the quarterback must be sure to drive the ball with his chest to the zenith point in order to provide maximum power and to prevent back-foot throwing. By throwing through to the zenith point with all the proper follow-through action, the ball will fall nose-down with proper trajectory and distance. Proper body follow-through to the zenith point is shown in Figure 9-5.

Figure 9-5
Proper body follow-through.

PASSING ON THE MOVE

"Move-out passing," in this text, will refer to the action of passing on the run. This type of passing is typical on such passing actions as the sprint-out, the roll-out, and the bootleg. Actually, on any of these actions, the quarterback could also execute a set up pass; for example, sprinting out to a fixed launch point, stopping, setting up, and throwing. In this discussion, however, move-out passing will be limited to passing while moving.

The major concept of move-out passing is that the upper torso action must be separated from the running action of the legs. The action of the chest, shoulders, and arms should be the same as on any other passing action. Of course, this action would be the optimal move-out passing execution, which is often difficult to achieve under game conditions. However, it is what we strive for in practice and execution. The goal is that from the chest up, all throws should look and be alike.

143

The basic premise of move-out action is the quarterback's threatening of the corner. By getting outside the defensive containment, the defense is faced with the added threat of the quarterback running the ball. Once he starts his move-out action, either right away on a sprint out or delayed on a bootleg-type action, the quarterback must accelerate to the outside as fast as possible to break the containment, threaten the secondary, and get away from interior pursuit.

A major fault in move-out passing occurs when the quarterback starts cocking the ball too soon. In turn, this action enables the defense to pressure the quarterback from the inside, because the secondary can then play more of a cat-and-mouse game since the quarterback has reduced his corner threat by indicating "pass." Thus, the quarterback's first three or four steps, depending on the pattern used, should be taken at top speed with the ball carried in front of the sternum in a position to best accommodate the run action. He, of course, takes more top speed steps on a bootleg action away from the launch point.

On the fourth or fifth step, depending on the direction of movement and if the quarterback is right or left-handed, the ball is cocked, ready to throw. This cocking action is no different from the cocking of the ball in the set up position, with the minor exception that the ball is held slightly higher and the elbow is positioned slightly out and away from the body in order to help accommodate the running action. Thus, the passing shoulder is cocked in a position where it won't have to be moved back any farther for the throw. The strain of the cocking action is placed on the twisted stomach area, as the chest is faced toward the pass target. Sticking the chest out toward the pass target helps to gather the entire upper throwing action, as well as to put proper upper body lean into the forward arm delivery of the ball.

The upper torso must be ready to execute the move-out pass without the aid of the legs and feet. What is desired, ideally, is that the quarterback will be able to gather his feet to help adjust his body's direction to a point where he at least opens up his hips toward the target. Opening or facing the hips toward the target point will help the upper torso throwing action. The quarterback on the move should attempt to step toward his target with his left foot (for a right-handed passer) whether he is moving left or right, and then roll over that front foot as he throws, just as he would in a normal set up throw.

A common tendency exists for quarterbacks to fully extend their throwing elbows in a locking movement, since this action is awkward to execute in relation to the running action of the legs. This action is especially true when the quarterback is moving to the side opposite his throwing arm and has to pass back toward the inside instead of out toward the flank where his run action is threatening. When running away from the throwing arm side, such an inside throw toward the free-arm side requires a side-armed, spinning type of throwing motion in which the hand is supinated (opposite of pronated), with the thumb turning outward as the palm turns upward. Whatever the technique used, proper follow-through by pointing the index finger and locking or fully extending the elbow is paramount to the success of move-out passing. In addition, proper stepping action with the lead foot will greatly enhance the ability of the rest of the body to properly follow through to the target point for a right-handed quarterback (refer to Figure 9-6).

Figure 9-6
Proper stepping action by a QB with his lead foot.

HALFBACK OPTION PASSING

The throwing action for a running back on a run-pass option is no different than a quarterback's passing action in the move-out game. The running back must also learn to disengage the throwing action of his upper torso from the run action of his legs, and throw the pass in the same manner as a quarterback who is sprinting or rolling out. Since the halfback option is generally more of a supplemental play-action pass than a bread-and-butter play in the offensive scheme, coaches are usually reluctant to devote too much practice time to it. For this reason, it is probably better to find the one or two running backs who can throw most effectively and concentrate on practicing their halfback option passing techniques. The coach must also be concerned with the running back's ability to get the ball to a desired target spot, rather than just with the techniques used for throwing. The main focus should be simply on improving the running back's overall passing effectiveness.

The most important factor in this improvement is concentration on the passing back's follow-through techniques—usually the weakest aspect of the running back's passing action. It is important to make sure that the running back points with his index finger at the target spot at the moment he releases the ball and that the full extension of his elbow reaches a locked position after the ball is thrown.

In order for the halfback option pass to be successful, it is paramount that the halfback threaten the corner with his run threat outside the defensive containment. Just like the sprint-out quarterback who shows pass too soon and fails to effectively attack the corner, the running back who throttles down too early to set up for the pass invites interior rush pressure, as well as helping the secondary defenders to play a cat-and-mouse game, committing to neither the pass nor the run threats. The running back must be sure to sprint to the corner to sell the run action and must not show any pass action until he has broken the defense's containment. One effective technique to help achieve this objective is to have the back start his normal end-run course, then flatten out to create the run-pass option threat (refer to Diagram 9-1).

The running back need not feel he has to throw on the run in the halfback pass. If the receiver is open and the running back has time, he can throttle down and set his feet, or even set up, to improve his throwing action.

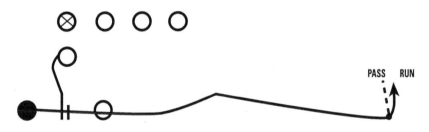

Diagram 9-1
North-south end-run course with flattening action
to accommodate a halfback option pass.

QUARTERBACK PASSING TECHNIQUES: PRACTICE AND DRILLS

Encouraging a quarterback to work on his passing techniques is about as difficult as prompting a baseball hitter to take a few extra turns in the batting cage. Passing is what most quarterbacks like to do best. Year-round practice can be accomplished with only a few resources—a football and an indoor area. A quarterback can even work by himself, if he has a number of footballs and a target as simple as a suspended tire or some sort of passing net. A minimal area can still allow all of a quarterback's drop-back or move-out actions.

Finding someone to throw to is also usually easy. Receivers like to catch the ball. Running backs rarely balk at working on their pass catching and route running skills. The quarterback, therefore, can easily work on his passing skills year-round. This situation is very desirable, because passing skill development needs quantity as well as quality. A sufficient "quantity of quality" repetitions best help to develop strength in the throwing arm, set up techniques, ball delivery, follow-through, and trajectory or "touch" passing, as well as timing with the receivers' routes.

As usual, drills for developing passing skills must be as game-like as possible. Practice of the move-out passing game, for example, should have the quarterbacks throwing to receivers running routes that are part of the offense. If the design of the play is to have the quarterback throw the ball on a timing pattern coordinated with a flanker's ten-yard out cut, then that total action should be practiced when the quarterback practices his move-out passing action. If the design of the pattern involves reading the secondary's movements or reading the receiver's cut, then these defensive/receiving situations should confront the quarterback and receivers in the drills used. Working with a center whenever possible also helps to coordinate the entire sequence associated with all passing actions, as well as helping provide further practice work on the important center-quarterback exchange.

Drill #1: Warm-Up

The warm-up drill is one of the most important drills to utilize each day. Warming up can be accomplished with two quarterbacks slowly throwing a ball back and forth for an extended time period. Quarterbacks can never warm their arms up enough. Usually they are not allowed enough time to do so. They should get to practice as early as possible to afford maximum warm-up time. In the warm-up drill, two quarterbacks stand ten yards apart and warm up their arms by throwing in their proper overhand manner. They practice vertical accuracy by trying to bisect the opposite quarterback down the middle of his body. Initially, they should not worry about pinpoint horizontal accuracy. As the drill progresses, and as the arms begin to warm up, horizontal accuracy may be added as an element of the drill. Diagram 9-2 shows the drill.

Coaching Points: The emphasis of the drill must be on gradually working up from slow, soft throwing to hard throwing. In this situation, many quarterbacks tend to be sloppy in their footwork, since they are "just warming up their arms." However, they must understand that they are warming up to develop their entire throwing motion. In a game, they will tend to throw as they have practiced.

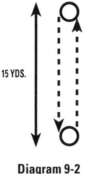

Diagram 9-2
Warm-up drill.

Drill #2: Double Kneel Throw

The double kneel throw drill helps develop the concept of separating the upper torso throwing action from the lower body running action, as in move-out pass action. Even if move-out pass action is not utilized, this drill is very valuable since it helps to develop the importance of leading the forward throwing action of the arm with the chest, which, in turn, enables the quarterback to better understand the importance of the upper torso in the delivery and follow-through. This drill is set up similarly to the warm-up drill shown in Diagram 9-2, except that both quarterbacks kneel on both knees and space themselves about eight yards apart.

Coaching Points: The coach must be sure to stress the importance of the quarterback's chest leading his throwing arm, so that proper thrust is added to the passing action by the upper torso. Another excellent variation is a one-knee kneel, with the knee opposite the throwing arm down. Putting the opposite knee down facilitates the best follow-through development.

Drill #3: Set up and Throw

The set up and throw drill helps develop all the proper set up actions utilized in the offense. The quarterbacks simply receive the snap from center and execute a proper drop-back and set up action and a proper delivery of the ball to a target or receiver. Complexity can range from throwing to a fixed target, to timing a specific pass to the cut action of a receiver's route, to creating one-on-one or two-on-two receiver-defender modified pass scrimmages. This drill helps develop proper drop-back action after a proper center-quarterback exchange, proper set-up technique, and proper delivery of the pass. Diagram 9-3 illustrates some of the various launch points from which the pass could be thrown.

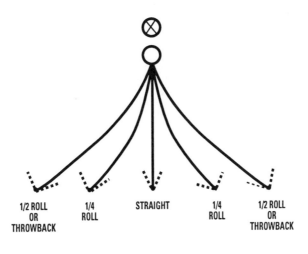

Diagram 9-3
Set up and throw drill.

Coaching Points: All of the various set up actions utilized in the offense must be practiced—drop-back, quarter-roll, half-roll, throw-back, and all play-action set ups. Such specifics as depth and speed of the set up, proper throttle-down on the next-to-last step, proper braking or stopping on the last step, proper set up and arm-shoulder cocking, as well as proper throwing action, should all be checked. Again, this drill can be performed with any combination of receiver route action and defender play.

Drill #4: Varying Foot Position

The varying foot position drill helps develop proper upper body throwing action, while separating it from the running action of the legs. It is set up like the warm-up drill with two quarterbacks facing each other at a distance of 10 yards. The throws, however, are made by placing the feet at various angles away from the straight line to the other quarterback (refer to Diagram 9-4). As these players throw from these various foot angles, they always turn their upper bodies toward the opposite quarterback.

Coaching Points: At the 135-degree angle, the trunk twist will be overly contorted. It will, however, help the passer to practice his upper body throwing action at its most extreme separation from his body.

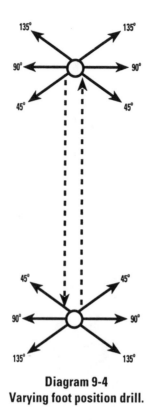

Diagram 9-4
Varying foot position drill.

Drill #5: Foot Adjustment

The foot adjustment drill is designed to enable a quarterback to develop quick, fluid feet, which, in turn, helps him adjust his set up to the receiver's route. From a set up position, the quarterback readies himself for a throw, with a proper ball hold and his shoulders cocked. A receiver runs a random, zigzag crossing pattern in front of the quarterback (refer to Diagram 9-5). All through the receiver's random pattern run, the quarterback uses quick, agile feet to adjust his set up to a target spot which will get the ball to the receiver. On a signal from the coach—"Now!" —the quarterback must have his feet set so he can immediately deliver the pass properly to the appropriate spot.

Coaching Points: The coach must vary the timing of his "Now!" signal for the throw, so the quarterback can perform proper foot positioning at all times while the drill is being conducted.

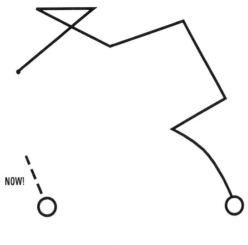

Diagram 9-5
Foot adjustment drill.

Drill #6: Move-Out Pass Ready

The move-out pass ready drill helps develop proper shoulder cock as the quarter-back is running. In the drill, the quarterback performs his normal move-out action–sprint, roll-out, bootleg–while a moving or stationary target is placed out in the flat. On the coach's signal, the passer must have his shoulder cocked properly, ready to execute a proper pass delivery on the move. Diagram 9-6 illustrates an example of sprint-out action.

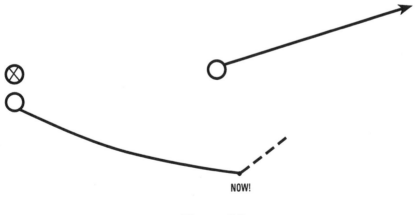

Diagram 9-6
Move-out pass ready drill.

Coaching Points: The coach must be sure to vary the "Now!" signal to ensure that the quarterback is cocked and ready to deliver the ball by the fifth step and on all subsequent steps.

Drill #7: Move-Out and Throw

This drill is set up just like the set up and throw drill, except that the quarterbacks perform all the move-out actions included in the design of the offense. It can also vary in complexity from throwing to a fixed target, to timing a specific pass to the cut of a receiver's route, to some type of modified defender-receiver passing scrimmage. It helps develop proper move-out passing action. Diagram 9-7 shows some of the various launch points from which the pass could be thrown.

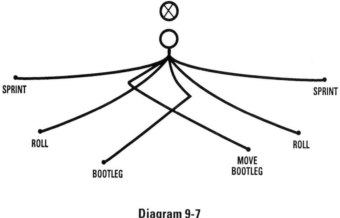

Diagram 9-7
Move-out and throw drill.

Coaching Points: All the various move-out actions must be practiced from both the right and the left. The coach must check the quarterback's efforts to properly threaten the corner, as well as all of the proper move-out passing techniques.

Drill #8: Trajectory Passing

The trajectory passing drill enables quarterbacks to practice various trajectory passing skills. Two quarterbacks start out standing 25 yards apart and practice throwing straight-line passes, high trajectory passes, and passes in between the two extremes (refer to Diagram 9-8). The passers continue the drill by increasing their distance by five yards at a time, until they work up to as much as 40 or 50 yards apart, depending on the arm strength of the quarterbacks.

Coaching Points: The number of repetitions at each 5-yard interval can be predetermined by the coach. However, each throw should alternate direct-line, high trajectory, and in-between throws. This passing sequence will help quarterbacks to develop a sense of the need for different trajectories for different situations in random order.

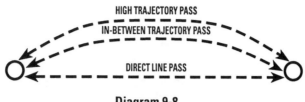

Diagram 9-8
Trajectory passing drill.

Drill #9: Deep Passing

This drill is designed to work on a quarterback's deep passing skills. From whichever launch points to whatever types of deep routes are utilized in their team's passing offense, the quarterbacks set up and throw. Complexity in the drill can vary from a simple timed drill in which the passer throws to a particular deep route of the receiver, to a complex modified pass scrimmage against defenders. It is important that the methods actually used by the offense to execute a deep pass be incorporated in the drill—timing, reading the coverage, reading the receiver, etc. Diagram 9-9 shows the drill being executed from drop-back action, in which the receiver is executing post, deep, or flag routes.

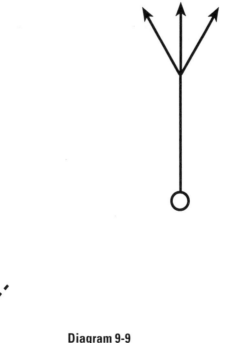

Diagram 9-9
Deep passing drill.

Coaching Points: The deep pass should initially be overthrown, making subsequent on-target adjustments to the receiver's speed relatively easy, since all the passer has to do is simply take something off the throw. This is far easier than initially underthrowing and then having to increase thrust and delivery effort. The passers must be sure to vary the trajectories of their throws. Quick timing must be emphasized. The passer must be able to "get the ball off" before the receiver outruns the quarterback's arm strength.

Drill #10: Skeleton Pass Scrimmage

This drill pits the quarterback, set backs, wide receivers, and tight ends against the secondary, linebackers, and ends. It is a competitive drill in which the offense executes all its pass offense against all the defense's pass coverages. Diagram 9-10 shows the offense in a pro-set skeleton formation and the defense in a 3-4 skeleton coverage.

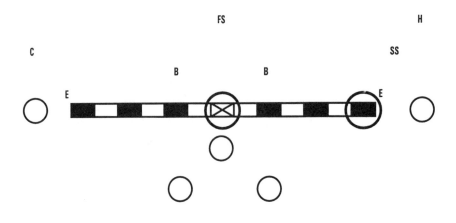

Diagram 9-10
Skeleton pass scrimmage drill.

Coaching Points: A center should be used to help create the proper sense of timing. A competitive game can be created by awarding five points for a deep completion or touchdown, three points for a medium distance completion, and one point for a short completion. The defense is awarded five points for an interception, three points for knocking down a pass, and one point for an incompletion or a pass that is not delivered within a set time limit. The coach should keep a stopwatch on the quarterback to ensure that the pass is released within a reasonable time limit (e.g., 3.5 seconds). Remember that this drill can be a defensive pass coverage drill, as well as a passing drill, which should help add to the level of competitiveness and game-like action of the drill.

CHAPTER 10

OFFENSIVE BACK RECEIVING TECHNIQUES

Writing a chapter on backfield pass receiving techniques is an extremely difficult task due to the overwhelming number of variables that must be considered. So much of pass receiving techniques for offensive backs depends on the designs of the pass patterns and the various assignments of the backs in the pass patterns. For this reason, this chapter will focus on general pass receiving and separation techniques and will provide practice drills for developing these techniques.

CATCHING TECHNIQUES

Catching techniques for a back are no different than for any other receiver. Five basic catching techniques exist: catching a ball above shoulder level, below shoulder level, over the shoulder, pocket catching, and one-handed catching. For all of these techniques, it is important for the offensive back to separate the catching action of his upper body from the running action of his lower body. In other words, one part of his body is running to place the other part of his body into the best position to receive the pass. The entire upper torso should be in a relaxed position to allow for a soft, cushion-like catch of the ball. The fingers should be well spread to form as wide a basket-like target as possible for the ball to fall into. Think of the fingers as pincers that softly engulf the ball to snatch it out of its flight path. The arms and shoulders should act as shock absorbers to lessen the impact of the ball, with the fingers enabling the soft catch. With a properly caught ball, no harsh, sharp, slapping sound of contact with the hands should occur. Instead, a soft catch should produce almost no sound at all.

A key factor in all five catching techniques is concentration. Concentration must be so great that the back should see his fingertips engulf the ball. Holding the hands well out in front of the body helps produce the hand-eye coordination needed for this to occur. In addition, holding the hands out in front enables the receiver already in position to actively "go get" the ball, instead of passively waiting for the ball to arrive and allowing the defenders an extra split second to make a defensive play on the ball before it is caught.

Catching the ball above the shoulders utilizes the thumbs-in technique, as shown in Figure 10-1. The thumbs should almost touch, while the other fingers should be well spread. The fingers really take on the pincer role in this technique. The hands must reach out for the ball, thereby facilitating good hand-eye coordination. The extended hands are in excellent position for the offensive back to actually sight the ball into his hands.

Figure 10-1
Thumbs in an above-the-shoulder catch technique.

Catching the ball below the shoulders utilizes the thumbs-out, pinkies-in technique in which the hands form a basket for the ball to fall into, as shown in Figure 10-2. This technique is similar to when the back receives a toss or pitch in a running play. The hand toward the ball forms the bottom of the basket, while the hand away from the ball forms the back-stop. The elbows should be fairly close together to facilitate positioning of the hands. The "back-receiver" must be sure that the fingers, and especially the thumbs, are hyperextended backwards, so they won't interfere with the ball as it falls into the basket formed by the hands. The receiver should raise the basket as high as possible to allow room for a soft, shock-absorbing, giving action in order to cushion the ball and produce a soft, secure catch.

Figure 10-2
Pinkies in a below-the-shoulder catch technique.

Catching the ball over the shoulder also utilizes the pinkies-in, thumbs-out technique, as shown in Figure 10-3. All of the catching skills are the same as for catching the ball below the shoulders, except that the back-receiver reaches up and out in front of himself to receive the ball in flight from back over his shoulder. A major effort must be made to catch the ball at the highest point possible, thereby allowing the receiver to see the ball right into his hands. If he allows the ball to fall to belt level, a blind spot is often produced. In this instance, the back's eyes are unable to follow the ball all the way into his hands.

When the ball is thrown low, at knee level or below, the offensive back may be forced to scoop the ball in an attempt to trap it to his body by using the pinkies-in technique, as shown in Figure 10-4. In this technique, a basket is formed with the fingers, palms, and insides of the back's forearms comprising the bottom of the basket, and the stomach and chest as the top of the basket. "Scooping" is an attempt by a receiver to get his hands and forearms under the ball before it hits the ground by using his fingertips to tip the ball upward and into the basket. Ideally, the ball becomes trapped securely in between the back's hands, arms, stomach, and chest.

Figure 10-3
Pinkies in over-the-shoulder catch technique.

Figure 10-4
Scoop technique to catch a low ball.

If the ball is close to the ground, the back-receiver may have to dive to the ground to give him his best chance of making the reception. When he makes the commitment to do this, he must be sure not to fall on his elbows, since doing so will tend to jar the ball loose. Instead, he must execute a rolling action as he hits the ground in order to lessen the jarring impact.

Because a pinkies-in catch is awkward to perform, the pocket catch is the best technique to use when the ball is thrown directly at the back. It is the safest and surest method for catching a pass, since the ball is almost totally secure upon reception. It is also an excellent technique for catching a wet ball. The pocket catch allows the ball to spin into the natural pocket formed by the armpit, the upper arm, and the side of the rib cage, as shown in Figure 10-5.

Figure 10-5
Pocket-catch technique.

In a pocket catch, the sides of the ball are actually trapped by the arm and rib cage as the nose of the ball wedges into the armpit. The receiver's hands simply engulf the ball and help draw it into the pocket so the ball is secured upon impact. The back must be sure that the fingers of both hands are spread and hyperextended away from the pocket, so they do not interfere with the flight of the ball into the pocket. Instead, the receiver's hands should form a funnel for the ball to enter.

The most difficult aspect of the pocket catch is body positioning. This factor involves lining up the "back-receiver's" catch-pocket with the flight of the ball. Depending upon the circumstances, he may have to speed up, slow down, or perhaps leap, to accomplish the pocket catch.

Whenever a pass is so far away from the body that a two-handed catch cannot be made, a one-handed catch technique is the only hope for a reception. In a proper one-handed catch, the receiver does not attempt to tip or bat the ball back toward his chest in an attempt to trap it. Instead, the receiver uses the one hand to form a one-handed basket which he then utilizes when attempting to execute a normal basket-like catch. As usual, the back's fingers should be well spread. The middle finger forms the backstop of the basket, while the thumb and the rest of the fingers are spread to form the sidewalls. The palm of the hand forms the bottom of the basket. The "back-receiver" must reach up for the ball. Similiar to the two-handed techniques, he must then use his arm to move his hand with the ball upon impact in order to create the cushioning effect. As the ball is being brought under control by the one hand, the other hand should be brought up to help secure the catch. If the receiver is forced to fall or dive to reach the ball, he must be sure not to fall on his elbows. Instead, he should roll upon contact to help absorb the blow and prevent the ball from jarring loose. The one-handed catch technique is illustrated in Figure 10-6.

Figure 10-6
One-hand catch technique.

THE IMPORTANCE OF POSITIONING

Positioning the body to make a reception is of utmost importance to the success of a pass play. The basic concept of proper body positioning is that the "back-receiver" must be under control so he can properly react to the flight of the ball, just as he must when he is about to deliver a forceful blow while blocking.

Correct body positioning enables the receiving back to properly separate his upper torso's receiving efforts from the lower body's running action. It is especially important that he keep his inside shoulder open to the quarterback to increase the range of his upper torso in its ability to react to the ball. Reacting, or moving to the ball, is also an important part of body positioning whenever defenders are behind the receiver. This factor cuts down on the defenders' time to react to the ball, as well as increasing the distance they have to move to get to the ball.

BACKFIELD RECEIVER SEPARATION TECHNIQUES

Separation techniques are those skills which enable a back to disengage from the man-to-man or zone coverage of a defender and become open to receive a pass. It is important to understand that the design of the pass pattern, the route the back is assigned to run, and the coverage he is facing will often dictate what separation technique he must use. Diagram 10-1 shows a weak side halfback isolation pattern in which the back executes a zone separation technique by throttling down or settling in an open zone void. The play is designed to use him as the prime receiver once he separates to get open off the movement of the pass coverage.

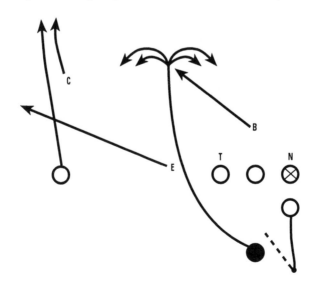

Diagram 10-1
Separate to get open vs. zone.

Diagram 10-2 shows how the same back would use a hard-driving man-to-man separation technique away from the man-to-man covering action of the same linebacker on some sort of man-under coverage. Instead of settling in an open zone void, the back either freezes the man-coverage linebacker and then breaks away hard to gain separation, or he breaks hard opposite the man-coverage if the man-coverage linebacker overplays him. It is important to note that on a man-to-man separation break, the back must sprint at top speed after he makes his separation move in order to maintain separation. He cannot settle into an opening after his man-separation has been accomplished, or he will simply allow the man-covering linebacker to catch up.

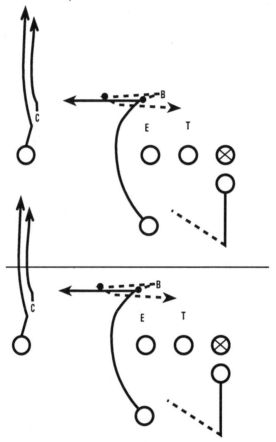

Diagram 10-2
Separate to get open vs. man.

Diagram 10-3, however, shows how the strict design of the flood pass pattern has the back running a strictly designed flat route of five yards deep with expansion as the major emphasis of the route. The design of this pass pattern attempts to create an open receiver by pitting two receivers against one defender.

Thus, strict placement of two receivers in two areas that cannot be covered by one defender is the key to the play's success—not the use of man-coverage type separation techniques to get open.

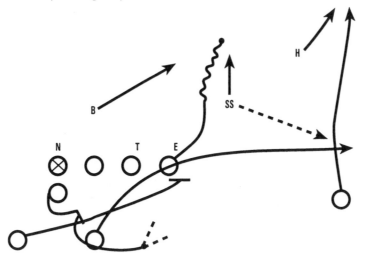

Diagram 10-3
Area assignment of routes to create a 2-on-1 mismatch
with no separation techniques.

The 90-degree angle turn-separation technique is one of the most common techniques used by backs, due to the fact that backs are often covered tightly by linebacker, in either zone or man-to-man coverage. The 90-degree angle turn basically attempts to redirect the back's movement from a north-south direction to an east-west direction. The separation technique is initially executed by bringing the body under control and taking a 45-degree angle step with the foot toward the side of the intended separation. The forward body weight is brought back so that a major portion of the weight is over the initial 45-degree step. The second step is both a break step and a plant step from which the third, or final, step is then initiated. The second step is a slight crossover step with which the cleats are firmly planted. The third step is now executed to finish the intended 90-degree turn by ripping the foot out straight toward the sideline and driving off the second, planted step. The 90-degree cut can be enhanced if the initial step is pushed at a covering linebacker or a defensive back in an effort to freeze the defender in place before the final phase of the cut.

The sharpness of the 90-degree cut is, or course, what helps separate the receiver from the defender. To execute such a sharp break, another common separation technique can be used. Snapping the head around toward the passer, as the elbow toward the quarterback is also whipped or snapped back toward the quarterback, helps to sharply disengage the receiver from the defender. This separation technique can be enhanced by the use of an opposite head-fake, or even by faking the 90-degree cut the opposite way before the actual cut is made.

Speed in itself is a major factor of separation. By varying his speed for specific separation actions, the back can have something left to help him disengage from a defender at the desired time. One such technique is releasing into a route at less than top speed. Showing a defender a less than full throttle release may enable the back to lull the defender into using a speed geared to that particular defensive situation. Then, a quick burst of speed on the back's final move will enable the back to disengage from the defender at the desired time. Releasing at less than full speed also enables the back to have his body under control, so he can best execute his final separation move.

Another popular speed separation technique is the change of pace. The concept, in this instance, is that when a receiver throttles down, he usually does it to execute some type of lateral or back-to-the-quarterback separation move. The defender reading the throttle-down action generally tends to cut down the "pad" of his coverage (i.e., the distance he keeps between himself and the back) and plays the back tighter. The change of pace separation technique is then executed by having the back shift his body backwards over a plant-type step, as the second step is dragged or suspended to influence the defender to think that a lateral or backward separation move is coming. Turning his head back toward the quarterback can help set up this influence. The third step, then, is simply an acceleration step back to full speed in an attempt to burst past the defender. At this point, it is important for the back to open up his stride to try to put more distance, or separation, between himself and the defender.

One of the most effective separation techniques is flat-out speed. This point is especially true when a speedy back is mismatched against a slower defender covering him. Deep or sideline patterns help to exploit such a mismatch. The back simply uses his flat-out speed to put distance between himself and the defender. Once that occurs, he then opens up to the passer. Too many backs will look up for the ball before they have truly separated from the defender, which only slows them down and gives the defender a chance to recover and catch up to them. This situation is especially true when the back-receiver turns his shoulders back to the quarterback, dramatically producing a natural slow-down of the back's run action.

Even after beating his man on a deep route, a back must maintain his speed when looking up for the ball. Any time a back slows down to look for the ball, he gives the defender a chance to catch up. Accordingly, he must continue to "burn" deep. In the same vein, reaching for the ball too early, fading too early, or closing in on the ball too early will also detract from the back's north-south separation. His major concerns must be to maintain full speed and to keep his stride stretched wide open, regardless of his upper body actions.

Another excellent speed separation technique is faking deep action by bursting deep before snapping off some type of lateral or back-to-the-quarterback separation action. Almost all secondary philosophies start with not getting beaten deep. Thus, the greater the north-south pressure by a speeding north-south receiver, the greater the retreating movement by the defenders to maintain their "pad." Setting a linebacker or secondary defender back on his heels with a deep threat, followed by some type of 90-degree cut, will usually produce a wide open receiver.

Another excellent separation technique is weaving. Often combined with speed separation techniques, weaving can be highly effective. The concept is to tightly attack one side of a defender—his hip—to threaten deep in an attempt to force him to turn his hips to allow himself to run deep with the receiver, who then breaks tightly off the defender's other hip. This action forces the defender to cross his legs and/or attempt a difficult crossover action, putting him at a great disadvantage if the back then opens up his stride and uses his speed to separate himself from the defender.

In this instance, tight weaving is the key. Too much lateral fake takes more time away from breaking back in the desired direction. As a result, the defender is given more time to react and stay with the back. The weave separation technique can be combined into a series of two or three consecutive weave moves to produce a sort of zigzag separation action. However, "zigzag" is a poor coaching term, since players often associate it with the more lateral action which should be avoided. The weave action needs to be kept tight and close to a straight-ahead path.

A come-back type of separation technique is executed similarly to the 90-degree angle turn separation. The major difference is that the third step off the second plant foot step is made in a sharper direction. Snapping the head and elbow will greatly aid this action, as will a greater degree of throttle-down, so that the back's body weight can be gathered over the first and second steps, thereby aiding the redirection efforts of the third step.

Against a defender who is playing the back tightly in a man-to-man or tight zone coverage, the shoulder drive separation technique is excellent. In this separation technique, the back tightly drives up north-south into the defender, similar to a faking-deep action, except that the back uses his shoulder to drive up under and through the defender to the spot where he wants to separate. This shoulder driving action is usually met with an effort by the defender to fend off the shoulder drive and maintain some sort of "pad." Such a defensive action, coupled with a separation action such as a 90-degree cut, usually results in significant separation.

An excellent complement to the usual 90-degree cut separation is the 270-degree cut separation technique, which is actually a three-quarter circle cut. The back sets up this move by driving at the hip of the defender opposite his ultimate cut to influence the defender to turn his hips in that direction. The back then throttles down to shift his weight back over his plant foot (i.e., the foot to the side of the intended cut). Next, he simply plants this foot and whips his opposite elbow back to execute a 180-degree-plus second step with the other foot. The third step is simply a crossover step with the original plant foot, thereby completing the 270-degree or three-quarter turn. The back then opens up his stride, starting with the crossover step, to put separation between himself and the defender.

Yet another effective separation technique is the use of a shoulder drag. In this technique, the back begins to turn his shoulders toward the quarterback to fake some type of lateral or backward move in order to influence the defender to throttle down, while the back continues speeding north-south.

Several other techniques can be utilized to put separation between the back and the defender. General concepts, such as running on a backpedaler and releasing on an angle against a defender moving laterally, can all be utilized to help the back separate from the defender in order to get open to receive a pass. What is important for the coach and the backs to realize is that any of these separation techniques can be used individually or combined into a series of separation moves. In addition, hand signals can be used effectively to tell a quarterback which way or when a back is going to break, to help develop pinpoint timing.

Specific pass receiving skills can also be associated with the various separation techniques, both to help the receiver to get open and then to react properly to the ball to make the reception. Fading inside or outside on a deep pass when it is thrown over the opposite shoulder is a difficult skill to master, since it involves quite an unnatural action. Proper practice, however, helps develop this important skill. Staying inbounds on the sideline or at the end line is another important skill. Another critical skill involves the necessity of a back who is stretching and reaching for a pass to be able to disengage the catching action of his upper body from the dragging action of the feet and legs. As his arms and hands stretch out to reach for the ball, the back must be able to make the catch. The use of peripheral vision as the back approaches the end line or sideline can help him adjust his body action properly.

BALL SECURITY AND NORTH-SOUTH KNIFING

As in any action which includes ball handling, ball security must be of utmost concern once the pass reception is made. Ball security actually begins with looking the ball into the hands and attempting to see the fingers engulf the ball. Next, the back's arms give with the ball to cushion its arrival, while drawing the ball into his armpit away from the upfield attack. The back should think, catch, tuck, and go. As the back develops a combined psychomotor pattern to execute the catch, tuck, and go action, the coach must be sure that the back secures the ball first and does not start knifing upfield before he secures the ball. When this sequence is fully developed, these actions will seem almost simultaneous. Ball security is a serious coaching concern, because violent tackles immediately upon reception are a common cause of the ball is being jarred loose.

Knifing north-south immediately after the reception is a critical factor in gaining yardage after the catch. A sharp north-south action is executed by lowering the upfield shoulder to initiate the turn. Once this redirection action is executed, the back must open his stride toward the goal line in order to put distance between himself and his pursuers to the rear and to allude any defenders in front of him with his north-south open field running techniques.

BACKFIELD PASS RECEIVING PRACTICE AND DRILLS

Pass plays in which backs are called upon to participate as receivers often produce a pass pattern's least efficient execution. Whatever the reason may be—lack of sufficient practice time, inadequate emphasis of the roles of the backs as receivers, etc., if the backs are the weakest receivers or the poorest at executing the separation techniques, the entire play will be weakened, because the defenders will be able to focus more attention on the other receivers in the pattern. Even though a back is usually a complementary receiver (i.e., not the primary receiver), he is no less important as a receiving threat. Studies of team reception statistics will often surprisingly show a back to be a team's second or third leading pass catcher. Why? Because deep zone coverages leave open the short zones that backs' routes often cross. Furthermore, man-to-man coverages frequently isolate quicker backs on slower linebackers. Coverages that concentrate on shutting off wide receivers, or the threat of a great tight end, will often leave the backs relatively uncovered. Whatever the reason, statistics show that backs play a far more active role in pass receiving than most coaches realize.

Keeping this in mind, pass receiving is still only part of the valuable role of a back in a pass pattern. A flood pattern, as shown in Diagram 10-3, can only be successful if the back performs a precise execution of his assignment. Whether it is a proper vertical or horizontal spacing of receivers, a crossing action, a flooding action, an isolating action, or any other combined action of two or more receivers in which a back is designed to fill a niche in the pattern, the back must execute his assignment precisely. This factor is true whether the back is the primary receiver, a complementary receiver, or simply designated as a decoy to influence or clear out a defender.

Realizing the limits of practice time and the need for developing precise running and blocking techniques, practice of the backfield pass game must be as concise as possible. Once again, the coach must go to the playbook rather than the drillbook. He must be sure to practice and drill those aspects of the passing game that his backs must actually execute in the offense used.

To make practice as game-like as possible, the coach should be sure that the backs thoroughly understand both their role in the pattern and exactly how to execute that role. Thus, each back must understand enough of the principles behind the design of the pattern to fully understand the purpose of his assignment. For example, "seam control," as shown in Diagram 10-4, refers to influencing the outside short zone defender to make him honor and play the halfback's seam control pattern. This pattern involves having the back run up the alley between the tackle and the split-end's weak-side out-route. The back must understand the importance of horizontal spacing, so that the outside short zone defender cannot cover both him and the split-end at the same time. He must also understand the importance of depth, so that he cannot be covered by a safety while the outside short zone defender covers the out pattern. Consequently, the back must understand why he needs to hold his seam control pattern whether he is covered or not. This understanding can do more to help the back execute his assignment than simply designating exactly where he should be and when. Knowing the reasons for these particular movements in a play can help the back to adjust appropriately to those abnormal situations that sometimes arise.

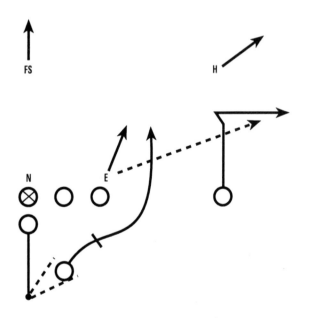

Diagram 10-4
HB seam control route.

Several of the following drills are pure pass catching skill drills. Other drills in this section are designed to enable a back to develop specific skills (i.e., running a particular route) that are integral to the back's execution of the passing portion of the offense by breaking down specific parts of the pass patterns into true game-like drills. For example, the boundary drill can be practiced and drilled off some type of square-out or flat route action that the back must actually execute in the pass offense.

Drill #1: Around the Clock

The around-the-clock drill is an excellent warm-up type drill which helps to check proper hand positioning, sighting the ball, finger pinching action on the ball, and arm-give for cushioning the ball's arrival. Two receivers stand about 10 yards apart and throw to each other to catch the ball at positions "around the clock," as shown in Diagram 10-5.

Diagram 10-5
Around-the-clock drill.

Coaching Points: Note that "X's" are drawn at the armpit areas so the backs can practice pocket catching. Throwing the ball at dead center also helps to create the pocket catch situation. The coach should check for proper hand positioning and finger spread, as well as the back's concentration on hand-eye coordination. The backs can finish the drill with "burn-outs"—firing the ball around the clock as hard as they can throw the ball. A contest can be made of the "burn-out." For example, how many catches out of ten throws or who is first to miss a catch? Another variation is to have the backs throw "knuckle-balls" to each other at the various points of the clock—an action that will help to develop the intense concentration needed to execute the "knuckle-ball" catching skill.

Drill #2: Spin

The spin drill is an excellent method to help develop quick catching reactions to a football that is not in the back's vision until it is right on top of him. In this drill, a back faces away from the coach at a distance of about 12 yards. The coach throws a hard pass at the back at any point around-the-clock, as in the around-the-clock drill. As soon as the ball has traveled about a yard from the coach's release hand, the rest of the backs in line yell "Ball!" This action signals the back to spin around and react to the ball and to make the catch wherever the ball is. The drill is shown in Diagram 10-6.

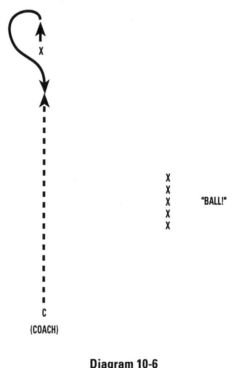

Diagram 10-6
Spin drill.

Coaching Points: The coach must be sure to vary his throws to different positions around the clock, including the armpits and dead center to force pocket catching. He must also be sure that the waiting line of backs does not signal the receiving back too early.

Drill #3: Catching on the Move

This drill enables the backs to practice catching a ball while moving across the passer's face or while running directly at the passer. The coach, or passer, must be sure to vary his throws, so the back can learn to adjust to the flight of the ball. Diagram 10-7 shows two actions—lateral and back toward the pass—off two possible routes the backs might have to execute.

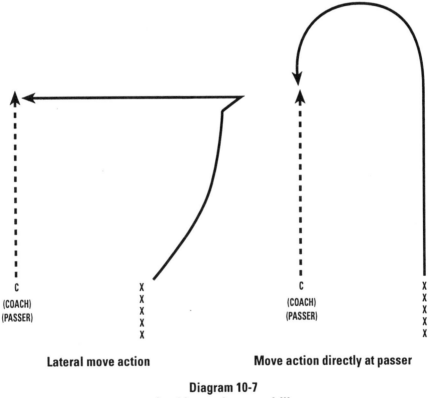

Lateral move action   **Move action directly at passer**

Diagram 10-7
Catching on the move drill.

Coaching Points: The backs must be sure to work both left and right. When working back toward the passer, the backs must learn to realize that the speed of the ball increases as they move toward it.

Drill #4: One-Hand Catch

The one-hand catch drill helps develop one-hand catching skills by forcing the back to concentrate on catching the ball and securing it under the armpit with only one hand. It can be executed by having the backs run either laterally across the field and directly at the coach (as shown in the upper part of Diagram10-8) or towards each flag and straight upfield (as illustrated in the lower part of Diagram 10-8).

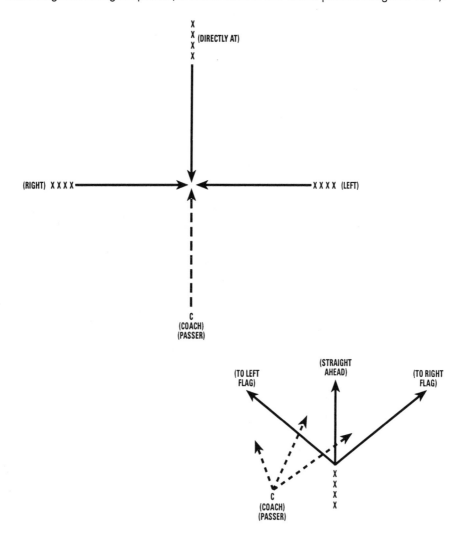

Diagram 10-8
One-hand catch drill.

Coaching Points: The coach should lead the back far enough with the pass so that the back must extend outward as in an actual one-handed catch situation in a game. The back should alternate right and left-handed one-hand catching.

Drill #5: Bad Ball

The bad ball drill is set up exactly as the one-hand catch drill, except that the backs practice two-handed catching of poorly thrown balls—too high, too low, short, long, wide, behind the back, etc. The backs must learn to be under control enough to enable them to react to a ball that is thrown off target. The backs must also learn that they need to do whatever is necessary to make the reception— dive, jump, lunge, etc.

Coaching Points: The coach should stress the ability of a back to keep himself under control, so that he can properly react to the ball. If the situation warrants it, drills such as catching on the move and bad ball can easily be combined into one drill to make better and more efficient use of practice time.

Drill #6: Dive

The dive drill helps the backs practice scooping balls that are low to the ground as well as proper rolling action, so that the backs do not land on their elbows where the ball could be easily jarred loose. The drill is set up similarly to the one-hand catch drill in which the backs work laterally across the passer. The balls are thrown very low in order to force the backs to execute their proper pinkies-to-gether scooping action. Diagram 10-9 shows how the dive drill can be practiced off an out-route action.

Drill #7: Deep

The deep drill helps the backs practice catching deep, two-handed, over the shoulder passes. The backs must practice both closing-in and fading adjustment techniques with the coach throwing the ball to either side of the backs, as shown in Diagram 10-10.

Coaching Points: The coach must be sure to alternate the flights of the ball, so that the backs can practice both closing in and fading skills. Extra emphasis can be placed on the more difficult fading action. The ball can also occasionally be thrown short in order to force the receiver to adjust back to an underthrown pass.

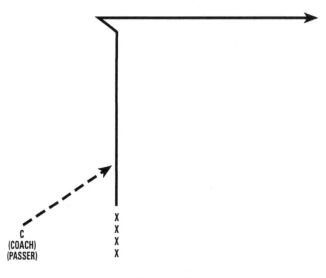

Diagram 10-9
Dive drill (off an out route action).

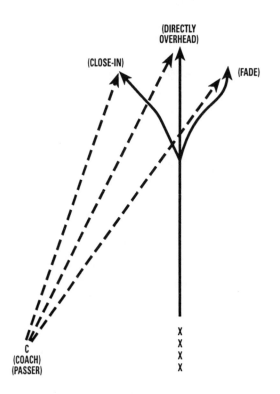

Diagram 10-10
Deep drill.

174

Drill #8: Pressure Drill

The pressure drill helps the back develop the concentration necessary to catch the ball in a crowd and hold onto it when the defenders hit him. It is executed by simply having the back run a particular route (e.g., the circle route shown in Diagram 10-11), while four extra backs wait for him in the reception area. When the ball is in flight, the extra backs try to distract the receiver with hand and air-bag waving actions. One extra back can even run in front of the receiver across the path of the ball. As soon as the receiver touches the ball, all the extra backs then slam the receiver with the air bag high and low in an attempt to jar the ball loose. One extra back can even drop the bag and use his hands in an attempt to strip the receiver of the ball.

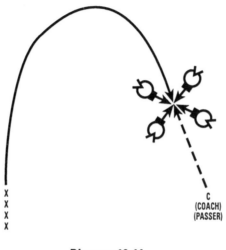

Diagram 10-11
Pressure drill (off a circle route action).

Coaching Points: Distractions as the ball is in flight are the key to this drill. A waving bag or even an air bag thrown into the air can help create appropriate distractions. The coach must check for proper ball security once the catch is made.

Drill #9: Double (or Triple) Hop

This drill helps the backs learn to catch the ball despite the potential interference of footwork problems. The back runs any of the short, across the field routes. Two or three bags are placed in his path about four feet apart, as shown in Diagram 10-. 12. The coach, or passer, fires a pass at the back anytime during his hopping the bags. The back must make the reception, while using the proper footwork to hop over the remaining bag(s).

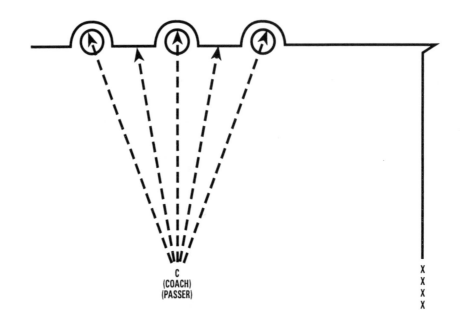

Diagram 10-12
Double (triple) hop drill.

Coaching Points: The coach must mix the timing of the passes to create different foot coordination problems for the back, as well as mix the varying flight angles of the passes—high, low, wide, behind, etc.

Drill #10: Boundary

The boundary drill helps the back practice his ability to make a reception and stay in bounds, whether on the sideline or the end line. The back sprints to the boundary, as shown in Diagram 10-13. For example, using a flat route to the sideline, he makes the catch and either knifes upfield or keeps one foot in bounds as he falls out of bounds.

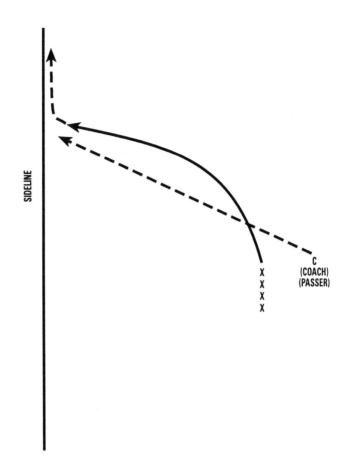

Diagram 10-13
Boundary drill (using a flat route to the sideline).

Coaching Points: The coach must be sure to practice endline boundary work as well as sideline. On the sidelines, the back must be sure to attempt knifing up the sideline if he can . It is important to stress the back's use of his peripheral vision, so he knows where the boundary line is as he approaches it, so he can maintain concentration and eye contact on the ball. The numbers on the field between the hash marks and sidelines are good cues to throttle down and come under control, so the back doesn't run out of room.

RUN BLOCKING

Backfield blocking is often one of the weakest areas of offensive play. The fact that backs are usually selected for their running ability, not their blocking ability, coupled with the number of different blocks the backs must master, is usually the primary cause of the inability of the offensive backfield to block effectively. However, if optimum offensive execution is to be achieved, backfield blocking must also be a strength. For example, the off-tackle kick-out play in which a 3-4 defensive tackle is eliminated by an excellent double-team block by the tackle and tight end is negated if the blocking back doesn't effectively execute his kick-out block.

The only way effective backfield blocking can be developed is to make it a high priority. The backs must be convinced that they can't be truly good backs if they aren't also good blockers. A coach could even go so far as to stipulate, "If you can't block, you can't play." In reality, however, such a philosophy may be easier to voice than to carry out, due to personnel limitations. Certain backfield sets may enable the weaker blocker to be placed in a position where he won't have to block as much (e.g., the "I" formation tailback spot). Another possibility is to substitute a strong blocking back for a weaker blocking back when a particular backfield position is assigned a key blocking assignment. This concept, however, has its limitations, since it creates a relatively easy to spot defensive key.

Frequently, a back is at a size disadvantage relative to the defenders he is assigned to block. He can, however, combine his speed advantage with an element of surprise (i.e., knowing ahead of time whom and how he will block, while the defender doesn't know who will block him, when, or with what technique) to help nullify the defender's size advantage. In addition, the backs are often among the best athletes on the field. Since blocking is as highly skilled a fundamental as any other football technique, a back can often rely on his extraordinary athletic ability to help him execute his blocking assignments.

This chapter concentrates on backfield run blocking techniques. It will not cover blocking concepts particular to a specific offense. Instead, the various types of techniques necessary to execute all such specific concepts will be the primary focus of this chapter.

THE ISOLATION BLOCK

The isolation block derives its name from the fact that the line's blocking scheme is designed to isolate the linebacker, or leave him alone, so that a back can block him one-on-one. The keys to the isolation block are an explosive and aggressive take-off and approach, use of the "freeze" technique by the ballcarrier, and an attitude of forcefully "making it happen!" The blocking back explodes from his stance in a low and powerfully gathered approach. His elbows should be kept in close to his body to avoid standing up and wasting motion. He aims at a point that is dead center on the linebacker, just below his shoulder pads. As a result of the ballcarrier's "freeze" technique, discussed in Chapter 7, the isolation blocker doesn't have to fear over-aggressiveness. Instead, he can "take it to" the linebacker with maximum speed and power to "make it happen." Diagram 11-1 shows two examples of isolation plays that utilize the isolation block from two different backfield sets, against two different defenses.

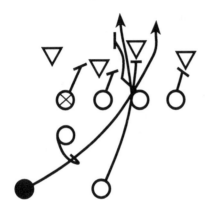

Diagram 11-1
Examples of an isolation block from split back and "I" sets.

The isolation block is executed by ripping up through the center of the linebacker with contact under his shoulder pads, just as the blocker is "stepping on the linebacker's toes." This contact is an attempt to punch up under the shoulder pads simultaneously with the palms of his hands. As contact is made, the blocking back arches his back and rolls, or snaps, his hips up under himself to help start the proper follow-through.

It is extremely important for the back to throttle-down slightly, just before he delivers the blow of the block. This action helps him bring himself under control, drop his tail, and widen his base, so that he is in a powerful and balanced stance from which to deliver his block.

The contact spot just under the shoulder pads allows the lifting action of the follow-through drive. In his follow-through, the back attempts to drive up through the linebacker's upper torso, as if the blocker were trying to lift him, or to drive him skyward at a 45-degree angle. Regardless of whether the ideal lifting situation exists (i.e., where the blocking back can totally control the linebacker), the blocker must at least attempt to drive the linebacker north-south by maintaining the press of the block.

An important coaching point is that contact and follow-through should be thought of as one continuous action. It is not rip and then drive. Instead, it is one simultaneous action in which the blocker attempts to blow through the linebacker to rip up through him at the desired 45-degree lifting angle.

All the body action of the back is predicated on a north-south thrust of his body power, with all body parts working straight upfield. He must be squared up with the linebacker so that the power in the thrust of the block is not reduced. Any turning of body parts off this squared-up plane (e.g., dropping or turning the head or shoulder, or twisting the torso) only reduces the back's blocking surface.

If, upon contact, the linebacker goes backwards, the isolation blocker continues driving up his center to prevent the linebacker from regaining his base. If, however, the linebacker slides to one side or the other, the isolation blocker rips north-south through the opposite side of the linebacker's chest, while the ballcarrier cuts opposite the linebacker's direction. The emphasis on ripping up through the side of the chest opposite the direction of the linebacker's flow in a north-south direction allows for maximum power, thrust, blocking surface, and base. This action will forcefully wall off the linebacker's pursuit course. If the linebacker attempts to go under the block, he eliminates his own ability to get to the speeding north-south barrier.

The blocking back should never attempt to gain an inside-out or outside-in position on the linebacker in order to shield him from the ballcarrier. This kind of shielding action is extremely passive, thereby allowing little, if any, powerful contact, explosion, or follow-through. If the linebacker tries to pick a side prior to contact, the isolation blocker simply adjusts his course to rip through the side of the chest opposite the direction of the linebacker's pursuit angle.

If the linebacker tries to overpower the isolation blocking back in an attempt to run over him, the blocker must concentrate on hitting him sooner. The blocker must simply collide with the linebacker through the middle and up through his shoulder pads, rather than focus on any follow-through techniques. This action will produce a less effective isolation block, but will at least save the play by preventing the linebacker from jamming the blocker back into the ballcarrier.

Another important concept is that the back must not lunge at a linebacker who is retreating from the line of scrimmage in order to avoid contact. If the linebacker retreats in any manner, the blocker continues to attack him. The blocker does not attempt to deliver the blow of the block until he is "stepping on the linebacker's toes."

An alternative technique on an isolation block is to cut block—a technique that will be described in Chapter 12. The blocking back attempts to rip a low cut block, parallel to the ground, through the linebacker's groin area. This action is an excellent technique to utilize on a goal line isolation play, when the linebacker attempts to jump on the pile.

THE LEAD-DRAW BLOCK

The lead-draw block is similar to the isolation block in that it isolates the linebacker for the blocking back's block. It differs, however, in that it develops off a quick drop-back pass fake and that the running back is not able to use the "freeze" set up technique as in a true isolation play. Instead, the lead blocker may be faced with a multitude of possible blocking situations, varying from the linebacker who has bought the pass fake and has already dropped three or four steps into his pass coverage drop, to a linebacker who has read the play well and is plugging the hole, or to a fully blitzing linebacker. What is similar, however, is that the lead blocker, upon contact, will execute the same technique on the lead-draw block as on the isolation block.

The lead blocker's initial movement is to quickly fake a pass-block set up by lifting into a two-point pass-block stance and immediately locating the linebacker he is assigned to block. After his initial quick lifting action to fake pass-blocking, the lead blocker explodes at the isolated linebacker and executes the appropriate isolation block technique according to the linebacker's reaction.

If the linebacker moves out into a pass drop and has positioned himself out toward the hook-curl zone area, the lead blocker will use a much more controlled type of isolation block, attempting to wall the linebacker out in the direction to which he has flowed, as shown in Diagram 11-2. The lead blocker attacks the linebacker using his normal, low, powerfully gathered approach, while maintaining elbows tight to the body to avoid any standing-up, wasted motion. His aiming point is to the inside of the linebacker's chest.

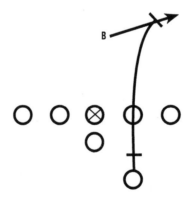

Diagram 11-2
Lead-draw blocking action vs. linebacker dropping to hook-curl zone.

As he approaches the linebacker, the lead blocker is careful to bring himself under control in order to be sure he does not over-extend or lunge into the block. He must remember that the linebacker is the person out of position in this case. All the lead blocker really has to do in this situation is keep his body between the linebacker and the ballcarrier. An isolation-type block is still used, however, instead of a stalk-type block, because linebackers are usually the type of players who have the physical tools to overpower a stalk block. In this case, the lead blocker is more concerned with proper contact than he is with follow-through, since such action is all that is needed to wall off the linebacker's pursuit to the ballcarrier.

If the linebacker drops back over the middle short zone area, as shown in Diagram 11-3, the lead blocker treats the action as that of a retreating defender. He attacks the linebacker's middle, while not breaking down in preparation for the ripping upward action of the isolation block until he can "step on the linebacker's toes." Once the blow is delivered, the lead blocker drives up through the linebacker's chest in a direction opposite the linebacker's effort to get to the ballcarrier, while maintaining his usual north-south follow-through.

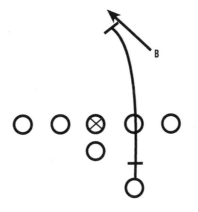

Diagram 11-3
Lead-draw blocking action vs. linebacker dropping to the short middle zone.

If the linebacker doesn't buy the pass fake and sits in his original alignment, the lead blocker executes a normal isolation block. The only difference between this action and the normal isolation block is that the ballcarrier can't help set it up with his "freeze" move, since his approach to the linebacker is not directly in line with the lead blocker's approach. This situation occurs because the ballcarrier is usually breaking off the block of a covered lineman, rather than the isolation block. As a result, the lead blocker has to be a bit more cautious and cannot "sell-out" as aggressively on his lead-draw block. He must avoid lunging out at the linebacker, who side steps in an attempt to set up and make the tackle.

If the linebacker blitzes, the lead blocker executes the same type of technique as he would on the isolation block. He breaks down sooner on his approach and thinks more about colliding with the linebacker through the middle and up under the linebacker's shoulder pads than about the follow-through action.

If the linebacker crosses the face of the lead blocker in an attempt to pursue the ball, as shown in Diagram 11-4, the lead blocker rips through the opposite side of the linebacker's chest (in relation to the direction of the linebacker's flow) in the same north-south manner of the isolation block. This technique attempts to blow the linebacker across the hole by taking him in the direction he wants to go, similar to the isolation block used on a linebacker who chooses a side in his attempt to get to the ballcarrier.

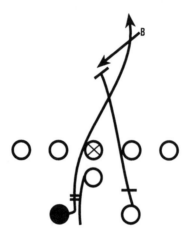

Diagram 11-4
Lead-draw blocking action vs. a linebacker who crosses the face of the blocker to get to the ballcarrier.

THE KICK-OUT BLOCK

The kick-out block is executed on the defensive end (or the end defender on the line of scrimmage). This block involves "kicking the defender out" to create an inside running lane in which the running back can cut up inside between that defender and the blocker. This action is shown in Diagram 11-5, in which the kick-out block provides an off-tackle run lane.

The key to this block is an explosive take-off and attacking the defensive end with speed and aggressiveness before he has time to read and react to the play. It is obvious to a blocking back that a physical mismatch often exists between himself and the defensive end. If the blocker takes advantage of his speed, technique, and the element of surprise, however, he can effectively execute the kick-out block.

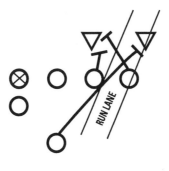

Diagram 11-5
The kick-out block.

The blocker should remember that he knows on what count the play will start, where the point of attack is, and whom he is going to block; whereas the defensive end knows none of this information. Herein lies the blocker's advantage. The defender must initially take time to read the play action to determine his appropriate reaction. In addition, the defensive end is often given "jamming" type assignments on the tight end at the same time he is trying to make his read. At best, his first few steps are shuffle or jabbing-type steps as he attempts to jam and/or read and still be in a position to react to all possible situations. Thus, the blocker, by exploding out of his stance at maximum speed directly at the defensive end, can burst into the defensive end with his block before the defender can charge forward. Thus, the size and power of the defensive end can be overcome.

The actual execution of the kick-out block is accomplished by having the blocker explode out of his stance and attack the defensive end at top speed with a low, gathered, explosive carry of the body. The most important concept on the take-off is to take an inside-out route, as shown in Diagram 11-5, to ensure that the blocker will be able to execute the inside-out blow necessary to produce a kick-out block. Keeping the elbows in tight will help produce a tightly gathered, powerful approach and help the blocker avoid standing up. The block is delivered by ripping up through the inside part of the defensive end's chest. The techniques for contact and follow-through are the same for the kick-out block as for the isolation block. The blocker uses the same north-south punch and press of the block.

Actually, the proper terminology for the thrust of the block is "north-south to the flag." Therefore, once the kick-out blocker makes contact up under the shoulder pad of the inside part of the defensive player's chest and continues on a north-south follow-through drive to the flag, he will cut off the defender's ability to pursue the ballcarrier. Even if the blocker doesn't cut off the pursuit angle, a continued press by the blocker with the proper follow-through should enable the ballcarrier to escape up inside the block as he runs tight to the double-team block on the other side of the run lane.

Another important reason for the inside-out approach to the kick-out block is that it allows the blocker to form a good base upon contact. A poor inside-out approach often causes the blocker to use a cross over step, thereby compromising the solid base necessary for a successful block since the blocker's feet will be one in front of the other upon contact. Proper and improper approach angles and footwork are illustrated in Diagram 11-6.

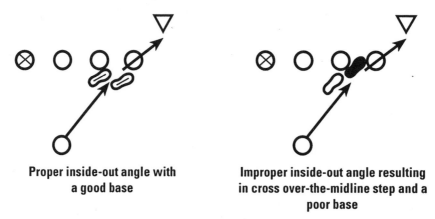

Proper inside-out angle with
a good base

Improper inside-out angle resulting
in cross over-the-midline step and a
poor base

Diagram 11-6
Proper and improper kick-out approach angles and resulting bases.

Defensive movement after the snap of the ball can cause two major variations in the kick-out blocking action. The first is when the defensive end closes down hard, thereby making a kick-out block virtually impossible due to the angle of attack with which the blocker is left with. When this happens, the kick-out blocker simply attempts to add thrust to the play by blasting over the top of the defender in an effort to "make it happen." This aggressive action is the best reaction to such a defensive maneuver, instead of hesitating, slowing down, or attempting to execute the kick-out without the proper inside-out angle.

The other defensive reaction to the kick-out block is a hard inside slant charge by the defensive end, thereby resulting in a lock-on action by the tight end in his down blocking assignment. If this occurs, the kick-out blocker hugs the lock-on action tightly and continues upfield in an effort to find a defender to block and to add thrust to the play. This defender will often be a pursuing inside linebacker. This situation is illustrated in Diagram 11-7.

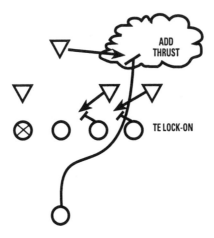

Diagram 11-7
Hard inside slant charge by a defender to be kicked
out, which results in a tight end lock-on action.

THE FAKE AND BLOCK

The fake and block technique is just what the term implies. A back fakes a ball-carry, as discussed in Chapter 6, and in one fluid motion continues on to block a defender. He fakes the carry off of some type of inside run action and maintains the fake-carry arm press against his body until he is "stepping on the toes" of the defender he is assigned to block. What the individual executing the fake should realize is that a convincing fake carry will make his second job much easier. If, as a result of the selling fake, the defender commits to the fake carry and tackles the faker, the block is unnecessary, because its objective is already achieved—taking the defender out of the play.

The techniques of the actual block at the end of the fake and block action can vary greatly. Which technique is finally used is determined by such factors as which type of play is utilized, the faker's position relative to the position of the defender to be blocked, and whether the play is a run or pass.

The first fake and block technique is the crash technique in which the back holds his faking course and does not veer off it to improve his blocking angle on the defender. Instead, he relies on a convincing fake to hold the defender in alignment, and then crashes into whatever piece of the defender is in his unwavering path. He may very well find that this action will by itself seal the defender inside or outside, as desired. Or, the blocker may find himself crashing through the defender's inside leg on an outside run play. However, if the fake is convincing enough and the crash is solid enough, sufficient contact will be made to slow the defender sufficiently to significantly hinder his ability to pursue the ballcarrier.

Another fake and block technique is the legal clip. As the back comes out of his fake, he pursues the assigned defender until he is "stepping on his heels." Once he is in this position, he simply drives the closest shoulder down through the back of the defender's knee area in an attempt to collapse the defender's legs. Once the defender is on the ground, the blocker must whip his inside elbow tightly up and out toward the sideline to propel his body into a series of three rolls over the defender's back, so that he can't regain his balance and get up to pursue the ballcarrier. The blocking back may also find it easier to crab block the defender to prevent him from regaining his balance and pursuing the ballcarrier.

The shoulder drive technique (which is another type of a fake and block technique) is just the opposite of the crash technique. The faker breaks out of his inside run fake course to get a good inside-out or outside-in positioning on the assigned defender. The same north-south thrust as in the isolation block is utilized. The blocker drives his head in front of the pursuing defender, catches him in the "V" of his neck and blocking arm, and drives north-south. Continued north-south follow-through and maintenance of the press of the block will seal the defender off from the ballcarrier.

If the blocker finds that the defender has pursued toward the ballcarrier too quickly to use any of the aforementioned techniques, he must pursue the defender until the defender breaks down in an effort to initiate contact. The blocker then drives the defender in the direction of his pursuit, across the face of the ballcarrier's path. If the blocker has already made contact, but can't seal off the defender's pursuit, he must maintain the press of the block and attempt to drive the pursuing defender across the face of the ballcarrier's path. In this manner, the ballcarrier will be able to break to daylight off this action.

On pass plays, the fake and block action faces the problem of an offensive interference penalty if the blocker makes contact more than one yard past the line of scrimmage. In this case, the crash technique is usually the best method, since a good fake is a prerequisite to the success of a good play-action pass, although the legal clip technique could be used. The major concern, then, is to be sure that the blocker plants a foot short of a yard past the line of scrimmage to halt his forward motion so he doesn't make contact and commit a penalty. A good teaching technique is to tell the back that when he is in doubt about being beyond a yard, "stop"—he probably is. Another alternative is to just continue through the line of scrimmage with a convincing fake, while looking to avoid illegal down field contact.

THE LEAD BLOCK

The lead block, or the direct block by a back on an interior lineman with little or no faking, takes on characteristics of both the fake and block action and the cut block, that will be discussed in Chapter 12. The lead block's main difference from the fake and block is that the back is selling out for the block at the expense of the fake. Little difference exists between the lead block and the cut-down block. The same cut-down block technique that will be discussed in Chapter 12 may be utilized as one of the techniques to execute the lead block. Thus, the lead block can utilize the crash and legal clip techniques of the fake and block or the cut-down block to eliminate an interior defensive lineman.

THE ARC BLOCK

The arc blocker is the first element of a two-man tandem unit in which a speeding ballcarrier is positioned just behind a blocker in an effort to get the ball to the outside, as on some type of sweep or option. The ballcarrier does not trail the arc blocker. Instead, he is positioned off the arc blocker's outside hip one-yard by one-yard, in order to make it difficult for a defender to pursue him because of the shielding action of the arc blocker. The ballcarrier is like the arc blocker's 45-degree "shadow," as they run like two jets in formation. It is important that the ballcarrier be taught that he must remain in that position until the actual contact of the block is made, so that the blocker has the opportunity to set up a successful arc block.

      The basic premise of the arc block is that if the arc blocker runs a proper arc-shaped course, thereby forcing the defender to come to him, and if the ballcarrier and arc blocker remain in their proper spatial relationship, then the defender cannot make the tackle. If the defender tries to come in from behind, the arc blocker takes his block up sharply into the defender as the ballcarrier escapes to the outside. If the defender fights through the arc blocker's head, the defender actually sets up the best possible situation for the arc blocker. If the defender over-commits to the outside while fighting through the arc blocker's head, the ballcarrier can cut upfield under the block. If the defender forces the arc blocker so far to the sideline that a running lane cannot be assured or if the defender's penetration is so deep that the arc block cannot be executed, a reverse hip technique off the normal arc block action is utilized as the ballcarrier cuts up inside. Diagram 11-8 shows the proper arc blocker-ballcarrier relationship.

      The initial course of the arc blocker is extremely important. He must start his course toward a point where the line of scrimmage intersects the sideline. This action enables the arc blocker to shield *any* possible pitch support defender within his arc course. Once the pitch or sweep support defender has been identified, the arc blocker simply shapes his arc to a course where the blocker's inside shoulder intersects the defender's outside knee. Upon contact, the arc blocker bends upfield at a 45-degree angle to maximize his blocking surface and power in order to achieve a tight fit on the block. The arc blocker *must* strive to achieve the

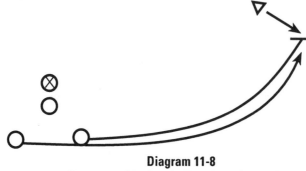

Diagram 11-8
Proper arc blocker-ballcarrier relationship.

arc block at all costs until the extremes of either being too close to the sideline or too deep in the backfield exist. The arc block is thrown with a sense of the blocker's inside arm ripping upward through the defender while the blocker simultaneously attempts to drive his head in front of and beyond the defender. At the same time, the blocker turns his inside hip up into the defender to give the block a broader surface. The most important part of the block, however, is striving for the proper initial body positioning in order to seal the defender inside. An equally important factor in the arc block's development is that the arc blocker must not attempt to deliver his block until he is "stepping on the toes" of the pitch support defender.

If the defender is positioned too wide to the sideline or too deep in the backfield, the reverse technique off the arc block is executed by having the blocker concentrate all the thrust of his block into his hip, while he simultaneously whips his legs around the defender and upfield. This reverse technique comes directly off the arc block look to help set it up. The arc blocker attacks the defender as if he's throwing a normal arc block. However, the initial ripping action of the inside arm becomes a decoy, as his inside hip is simultaneously whipped around and his legs are whipped upfield in an effort to seal the defender out on the sideline.

The coach can teach definite cues for when to use the reverse technique off the arc block. When the assigned defender penetrates so deeply into the backfield that the blocker can no longer see his outside leg or the blocker would have to belly deeper to get to it, the reverse arc block should be used. Another instance when an arc block should be used occurs when the blocker feels that he is so close to the sideline (e.g., three to four yards) that his block on the defender will do nothing but clog the running lane up the sideline. Diagram 11-9 shows these two possible situations.

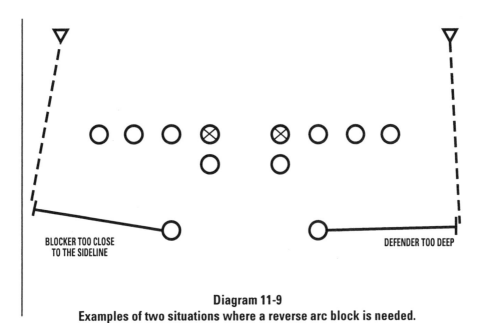

BLOCKER TOO CLOSE
TO THE SIDELINE

DEFENDER TOO DEEP

Diagram 11-9
Examples of two situations where a reverse arc block is needed.

Remember that the defender assigned to pitch support can come from many different alignments involving many different pursuit angles and from many different defensive actions. Walk-away ends, defenders in bump-and-go alignments on wide receivers, crash charges, and cross charges are all examples of the actions to which the arc blocker and the ballcarrier must be ready to adjust. The arc blocker has to take up the arc within the arc of the ballcarrier's path to get to the outside knee of the pitch support defender, no matter how sharp or acute that arc within the arc may be. Diagram 11-10 shows several examples of different arcs necessary to get to various contact points with the pitch support defender.

BACKFIELD RUN BLOCKING TECHNIQUES PRACTICE AND DRILLS

As in the practice of any other backfield skill, the coach must set up game-like drills that will help the backs develop the actual skills they will use in games. He must again go to his playbook and isolate segments of his actual offensive plays in order to ensure useful and necessary preparation. This situation doesn't mean that pure blocking drills will have no value. Any drill utilized, however, must help the players develop skills they will need to execute their assignments. Otherwise, the drills will be unproductive and waste valuable practice time.

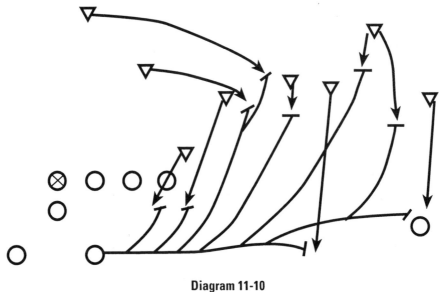

Diagram 11-10
Varying arcs taken by an arc blocker.

Drill #1: Board

The board drill helps develop an explosive stance and take-off, a wide base, and proper throttle-down movement in which the blocking back broadens his base by dropping his tail prior to contact and follow-through. It's an excellent preseason drill, when basic fundamentals are being taught or reviewed. This drill is designed to help develop the all-important drive block used on the isolation, lead-draw, and kick-out blocking assignments.

In this drill, a beveled board is used (refer to Diagram 11-11) in order to force the blocker to keep the desired wide base. The backs fire out, explode into the dummies held by other backs, and drive the dummies backwards off the board using proper follow-through techniques. As on all blocking action, the block is maintained until the whistle is blown. The players must be sure to practice drive blocking left, right, and straight ahead.

Coaching Points: All of the proper drive blocking techniques utilized in the isolation, kick-out, and lead draw blocks must be taught, with special emphasis on proper base, contact, and follow-through.

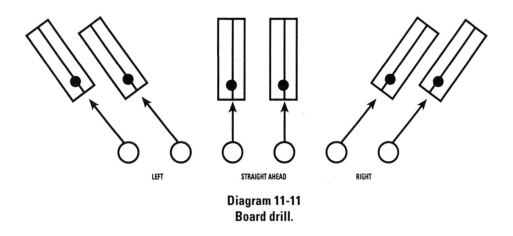

LEFT STRAIGHT AHEAD RIGHT

Diagram 11-11
Board drill.

Drill #2: One-Man Sled

The one-man sled drill helps develop the same skills as the board drill. Using a sled, however, enhances the practice of maintaining a proper base and body balance during contact and follow-through. A one-man drive block action on a two-man sled may be a more appropriate tool for teaching these factors than using a one-man sled, because a two-man sled requires greater coordination of body balance, contact, and follow-through. The backs should drive each side of the sled, in order to practice using both shoulders.

Drill #3: Isolation/Lead-Draw Block

The isolation/lead-draw block drill is designed to help develop the correct blocking techniques utilized on the isolation and lead-draw plays. Another back, or a linebacker to simulate a more game-like condition, holds a large shield. On the snap of the ball, or on the starting cadence, the player holding the shield executes one of the possible reactions that a linebacker could make to a blocker who is attacking him in a lead-draw or isolation play. Diagram 11-12 illustrates several possibilities.

Coaching Points: The coach signals to the linebacker what reaction to execute, and calls out which type of block he wants the blocker to use—isolation or lead draw. All points of proper execution of each block are checked. The coach must also be sure to vary the linebacker's reaction sequence for each blocker. The blocking backs must be sure to practice their blocks from both sides.

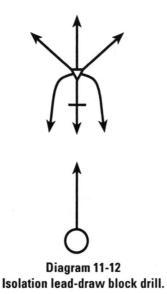

Diagram 11-12
Isolation lead-draw block drill.

Drill #4: Kick Out

The kick-out drill is set up and run much like the isolation/lead-draw drill. Another back, or a defensive end can be used to simulate more game-like practice, holds a large shield. On a signal from the coach, the defender executes one of the three defensive maneuvers that the kick-out blocker might face as he carries out his kick-out action. The drill set up (using a tape or hose on the ground to indicate proper alignment and positioning of the blocker and defender) and possible end defender reactions are shown in Diagram 11-13. The backs must practice blocking to both sides.

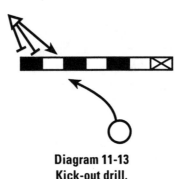

Diagram 11-13
Kick-out drill.

Drill #5: Fake and Block

The fake and block drill is also set up similarly to the isolation/lead-draw block drill and the kick-out block drill, except that a heavy bag is used to simulate a defensive lineman. All of the various techniques of the fake and block-action—crash, legal clip, shoulder drive, or driving the over-pursuing defender past the ballcarrier's run lane—are practiced against all the various reactions that a blocker may see from the defender he is assigned to block. The various reactions a blocker might encounter are illustrated in Diagram 11-14.

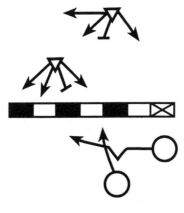

Diagram 11-14
Fake and block drill.

Coaching Point: A quarterback could be used to help practice the fake.

Drill #6: Lead Block

The lead-block drill also simulates all the possible techniques and defensive reactions that might occur on a lead blocking assignment. A heavy bag is used to simulate a defensive lineman. The defensive reactions should be varied, and the backs should practice the lead block to both sides (refer to Diagram 11-15).

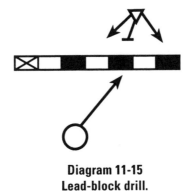

Diagram 11-15
Lead-block drill.

Drill #7: Arc Block

The arc-block drill enacts all the techniques and defensive reactions that might occur on an arc-blocking assignment. The back simulating the defender carries a heavy shield. The action, as shown in Diagram 11-16, must be practiced to both sides. In addition, this drill should involve a ballcarrier, since the relationship between the arc blocker and the ballcarrier is paramount to the successful execution of the block. This drill is also designed to help the ballcarrier practice his role as well.

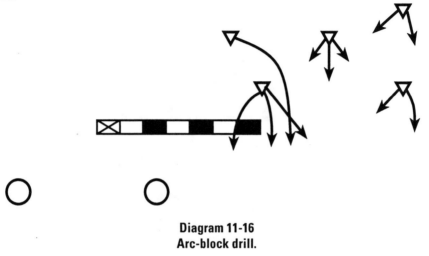

Diagram 11-16
Arc-block drill.

Coaching Points: As shown in Diagram 11-16, the back simulating the defender must vary both his alignment and his reactions. A strong safety, outside line-backer, or corner back type defender could be used without a shield to create game-like action. It is important that the blocking back be confronted with reverse arc-block situations also, to practice that skill.

Drill #8: Multiple Run Block

The multiple run block drill is an excellent rapid-fire drill that helps create a great variety of blocking assignments, defensive reactions, and technique execution. Pass blocking action can be added to create a multiple block drill. This drill, however, requires a large number of defenders to man the drill, and perhaps even a second coach. The drill sets up all the aforementioned situations—isolation/ lead-draw, kick-out, fake and block, and arc-block drills. Two backs work at the same time to accommodate more repetitions. A second coach can help position defenders and call for a variety of defensive reactions when the coach working with the blockers calls for specific blocking assignments. It is important to vary both the defensive alignments and the defensive reactions. Diagram 11-17 shows a possible alignment of the drill that can be varied according to the particular defense for which you are preparing. The numerous individual reactions of each defender are not diagrammed to avoid cluttering the figure, since they have already been shown in Diagrams 11-12 to 11-16.

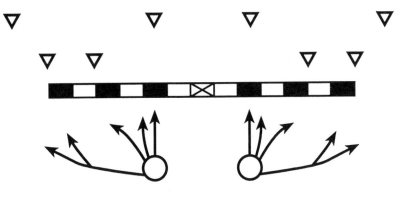

Diagram 11-17
Multiple run block drill.

Coaching Point: Interior defensive linemen are simulated with heavy bags, while all other defenders use large shields.

AUTHOR'S NOTE:
On most of these drills, it has been stressed that the backs practice their blocking to both sides. Actually, such practice is needed only if the back actually executes blocks to each side. If, due to the particular offensive concept, the blocker's backfield alignment remains constant, and he only blocks to one side, then he need practice his blocks only to that side.

CHAPTER 12

PASS BLOCKING

Two basic types of backfield pass blocking techniques can be developed and mastered—cut blocking and pass-pro blocking. Although cut blocking may appear to be a difficult technique, it can become a high percentage block for most backs. Once they get the hang of it, they will enjoy performing it because of its strategic effectiveness within the execution of the play and because of its demoralizing effect on the usually bigger and stronger defenders who are being cut down. Pass-pro blocking, however, may be a very difficult blocking task for backs to master. Since it is a more passive block, pass-pro blocking can compromise the few advantages a back may have in blocking larger defensive linemen—speed, explosive power, and surprise. Diligent effort and concentrated practice, however, can help backs develop into effective pass-pro blockers.

THE CUT-DOWN BLOCK

The cut-down block attempts to "cut down," or rip the outside leg or legs from under the first defender outside the tackle's block or the end defender on the line of scrimmage, depending on the defensive alignment and the type of blocking scheme called. A cut-down block is also commonly used to block a blitzing linebacker who is attacking forward at full speed. It can also be used as a run game block as a technique for the lead block (to block an interior defensive lineman), the load block (to cut down the end defender on the line of scrimmage on a sweep or pitch play), or the isolation block or sweep block (to cut a linebacker). Since they all utilize the same execution technique and are, in actuality, the same block, the discussion of the cut-down block has been saved for the passing game, where it is most commonly used. Diagram 12-1 shows three types of uses for the cut-down block.

On sprint-out or move-out type action, the cut-down block is used for a variety of reasons. It gets the blocker to the defender fast, with maximum blocking thrust and power, and keeps the block away from the launch point, thereby minimizing the possibility of disrupting the passer. The cut-down block also denies the defender penetration, forcing him to make a more lateral move to avoid the block. The more the defender moves laterally, the easier it is for the quarterback to see the defender's movement and adjust the launch point as needed. In addition, the cut-down block helps to keep the defender's hands down, thereby preventing interference with the pass, while the defender tries to fend off the low blocking action of the cut-down block.

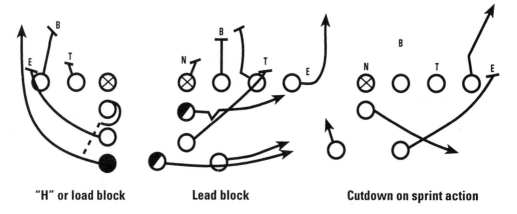

| "H" or load block | Lead block | Cutdown on sprint action |

Diagram 12-1
Examples of uses for a cut-down block.

The blocker must understand that the quarterback's action will, in itself, help deny the defender an inside rush route. Thus, the emphasis of the blocking action is an effort to gain outside leverage on the defender's outside leg, thereby denying the defender both penetration into the backfield and lateral movement, since the defender is actually sealed to the inside. Although such an inside rush route will create a tougher technique problem for the blocker, the blocker will be able to accomplish his task by directing his approach up into the inside rush of the defender, then utilizing a shoulder block to bump the defender off his course. If the defender chooses to go outside the block (i.e., attempt to go around the blocker), the quarterback will easily be able to spot him in his peripheral vision, adjust the launch point, and avoid him. If the defender attempts to jump over the cut-down block, the blocker can effectively protect the launch point. When the pass called requires the quarterback to move more than five steps to the outside, another back can be assigned to the outside knee of the rusher. Diagram 12-2 shows how the relationship between the quarterback and the cut-down blocker helps to deny the possibility of an inside rush in hindering the play's development.

In the execution of the cut-down block, an explosive take-off is of utmost importance. As in the kick-out block, the defender must initially read the offensive action to properly react to the block. In addition, the defender is often on some type of "jamming" assignment. Thus, the blocker, by exploding out of his stance at maximum speed directly at the defender's outside knee, has the ability to explode into the defender with the cut-down block before the defender can charge forward into the blocker. This action enables the usually smaller blocker to nullify and overcome the defender's size and power advantage.

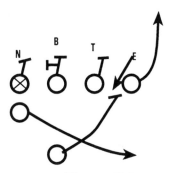

Diagram 12-2
Quarterback-cut-down blocker relationship denying an inside
rush from threatening the play.

The aiming point of the block is the top of the defender's outside knee. However, three things are paramount to the success of the block. First, the blocker must not attempt to throw the block until he is "stepping on the toes" of the defender. This requirement prevents the blocker from lunging out and/or losing contact. Second, the blocker must secure a "tight fit" on the defender by concentrating on driving his inside shoulder down through the defender's crotch and through the top of his outside knee to rip the defender's outside leg from under him. This action enables maximum blocking surface, contact, and power. Third, the blocker must rip the block north-south through the defender's outside knee. This action will in itself help to seal the defender to the inside.

The major cause of failure of the cut-down block is an east-west throwing of the block in which the blocker's inside shoulder and head end up being thrust toward the sideline, an action that enables the defender to play through the blocker's head to the outside, since the blocker loses both contact and power.

If the defender tries to get inside the blocker, the blocker just shapes his attack up into the defender, again in a north-south direction, and puts a shoulder into the defender to enable the quarterback to escape to the outside. If the defender moves upfield or outside laterally, the blocker must remember the cardinal rule of not throwing the block until he is "stepping on the defender's toes." Sooner or later, the defender will have to react through the blocker if he wants to attempt to rush the quarterback.

Follow-through via a rolling action is most important to the success of the cut-down block. Cutting a defender down is of little use if he is able to get up and continue his pursuit. In this rolling action, the point is to roll into the defender, to maintain contact as long as possible, and to keep the defender from regaining balance. The roll is initiated by whipping the outside elbow back into the defender immediately after the blocking contact. If the defender attempts to jump over the blocker after the block is thrown, the blocker must follow through by lifting or ripping straight up through the defender's crotch as the defender is jumping over or straddling the blocker. The cut blocker may also find that crab blocking helps to eliminate the ability of the defender to recover and pursue the quarterback.

When two backs are assigned to cut down one defender, two techniques can be utilized. In the first, the first blocker can set up the blocking by crashing downward through the center of the defender with a normal cut-down action, while the second blocker cleans up with normal cut-down action through the defender's outside knee. In the second technique, the first blocker attempts to cut down the defender alone, with his normal cut-down block, while the second blocker only "cleans up" if needed. Thus, the second blocker is available to block any additional defenders from the outside-in or the inside-out, especially a scraping linebacker.

Whether one or two backfield blockers are used, it is not uncommon for the defender who is to be cut down to drop off into pass coverage, thereby leaving no one to block. When this situation occurs, the cut-down blocking back must recognize this action as he approaches the line of scrimmage and should react as shown in Diagram 12-3. When the cut-down blocking back sees the defender drop off into pass coverage, he continues to a point out past the next blocker inside of his intended blocking target, wheels to the inside, and readies himself to cut-down block the first defender who comes free in pursuit down the line of scrimmage. This sealing type of cut-down block, in which he helps block a defender who has slipped off a teammate's block or a linebacker who is pursuing close to the line of scrimmage, is executed in the same manner as a normal cut-down block. The blocker's aiming point is the top of the outside or upfield knee of the defender who comes free.

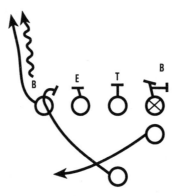

Diagram 12-3
Cut-down blocker turning inside to help once his
assigned defender drops off into pass coverage.

This blocker, who has now become a "sealing back," must realize that if he seals down to the inside on a defender who is already in contact with another blocker, he cannot legally cut-block. His seal block then will have to be above the defender's waist.

Two other points need mentioning. If the defender who is to be cut-down blocked feathers out down the line of scrimmage, and droped off only three or four yards off the line of scrimmage the cut-down blocker must slide along down the line of scrimmage and position himself between the defender and the quarterback, as shown in Diagram 12-4. In this way, he will be able to protect the quarterback if that defender decides to put on a delayed rush. If the cut-down blocker prematurely turns inside to help, and the defender puts on a delayed rush, the quarterback will be left unprotected. The key coaching point in this situation is that if the blocker is in doubt about what the defender is doing, he must always stay in front of the defender to protect the quarterback. The blocker must not leave the quarterback unprotected by turning inside to help.

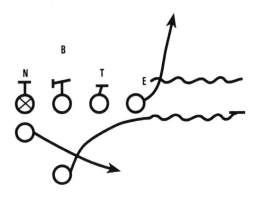

Diagram 12-4
Cut-down blocker staying in front of the defender who neither rushes
nor drops into pass coverage.

The second point is a continuation of the first. When the cut-down blocker finds himself in such a sit-and-wait situation (whether because the defender neither drops off into pass coverage nor rushes, or because the blocker has turned inside to help, thereby leaving no one to help on the cut-down), the back must be ready for a possible "Go!" call by the quarterback. The "Go!" call will allow the back to release upfield to run-block for the quarterback, who is now running the ball.

Another major problem of the cut-down block is that the cut-down blocker will often find that he is not able to get a tight fit in the block because the defender is feathering out away from him. As a result, the blocker is unable to rip out the defender's inside leg. This situation usually results in the defender's fending off the block with his hands in an attempt to keep his legs away from the blocker. If this happens, the back immediately switches to a scramble-block technique in an attempt to prevent the defender from regaining his balance to slip to the outside and pursue the play. The blocker tries to scramble into the defender's legs to tie him up until the play is over.

THE PASS-PRO BLOCK

Body positioning and a controlled delivery of the pass-pro block against the rusher are the keys to effectively blocking a rusher. First, the pass-pro back's body should be positioned between the oncoming rusher and the quarterback so that the rusher can't get to the quarterback. Pass-pro backs must be taught that utilization of proper pass-pro techniques will prevent the pass rusher from being able to go over the top of the blocker. If the rusher tries to go around the blocker, the "riding-out or riding-in" techniques will force lengthening of the rusher's route, thereby buying time for the quarterback. The backs must understand that their assignment is not to knock the pass rushers down or backwards, but to buy time for the quarterback. Each yard a blocker gives up grudgingly buys another second for the quarterback.

The pass-pro blocker initially sets up by stepping up and out toward the defensive end (i.e., the end rusher) to be blocked. (The pass-pro block will be discussed versus an outside rusher. Of course, the same pass-pro blocking technique can be utilized versus an inside linebacker.) This action should position him in the approximate area of the outside shoulder of the tackle, as shown in Diagram 12-5. A major teaching point for the set up is that the pass-pro blocker's rear end should "take a picture" of a spot one to one-and-a-half yards in front of the quarterback. This alignment will allow the pass rusher to see a rushing lane through the outside shoulder of the blocker, thereby inviting the defender to pass rush outside. The pass-pro blocker will, however, still be aligned so that his body is between the rusher and the quarterback.

The blocker's tail is sunk low to prepare him for the "standing-up-the-rusher" blow. The blocker keeps his elbows in tight to create a low and powerfully gathered stance. He holds his fists in front of his chest. He keeps his feet "floating"—ready to shuffle in any direction to maintain his inside-out alignment against the pass rusher's path to the quarterback.

The pass-pro blocker *must be patient!* If the pass rusher is slow in his approach, the blocker *must not attack!* It must be remembered that the pass-pro blocker's assignment is to buy time for the quarterback. If the rusher is slow to approach, the blocker must wait for him—buying time all the while. Attacking a slow rusher, or any pass rusher for that matter, will only cause lunging and overextending the block—death knells for a pass-pro blocker.

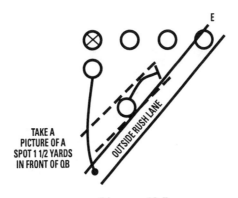

Diagram 12-5
Proper back pass-pro positioning for the end rusher.

The key to delivering the blow is for the blocker to explode at a point halfway between the rusher's center and the inside of his chest area, up under his shoulder pads, when the rusher is so close that the blocker can only see the rusher's number in his face. The blocker then slams or rips upward with the palms of his hands, his elbows extending up and away from his body, in an attempt to stand the rusher up and stop his charge. During this technique, the blocker arches his back and snaps his hips up under the pass rusher. As previously mentioned, the blocker should not attempt to blast the rusher backward, because when the blocker's weight is extended out forward, he is unable to maintain a press of the block until the whistle is blown. On the first blow of the block, an extra powerful, extended blow might be initially more successful, but it also will probably be the last of his efforts to buy time for the quarterback because of his being over-extended. In addition, the blocker must not straighten and lock his legs while trying to blast the defender upward, because from this position, he will lose his athleticism and not be able to slide in response to any lateral movement of the rusher and maintain a press of the block. Proper and improper deliveries of the pass pro blocking techniques are shown in Figure 12-1.

Proper set up

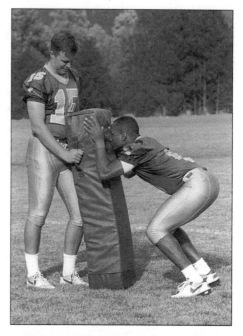

Proper delivering of the pass-pro blow

**Improper overextension of the
pass-pro blow**

**Improper straightening up and locking
of legs on the pass-pro blow**

**Figure 12-1
Proper and improper delivering of pass-pro blow techniques.**

Given the rule changes that permit the use of the hands in blocking, a coach may prefer to utilize a lineman's arm lock-out extension of the hands into the bottom outside of the rusher's numbers. The arm lock-out technique, as shown in Figure 12-2, allows for the back to keep his weight back and allows for the disengagement of the blocker's and the rusher's bodies. In this manner, the rusher is not able to grab the blocker's body as easily, thereby limiting his pass-rush abilities. In reality, however, the usually smaller back will find his palms, forearms, and chest pressed up into the usually larger rusher.

Figure 12-2
Arm lock-out technique.

Once the pass-pro blocker has "ripped up" into the rusher and has stopped his charge with the blocker's arms locked outward to keep the rusher off his body, he then presses himself into the movement pressure of the rusher. The pass-pro blocker constantly attempts to maintain his inside-out alignment to continue to encourage an outside pass rush by the defender.

Additional adjustments in techniques for handling different situations can occur when blocking the rusher. If the pass-pro blocker begins to lose the rusher to the outside, he should drive his head in front of the rusher in a sealing effort and ride the rusher out to the sideline. As a general rule, if the blocker realizes

207

that the rusher's numbers are beginning to disappear because the rusher is bypassing him laterally, he should seal block. The seal block is executed by bringing the "flipper" up to the side of the blocker's neck to make contact and to attempt to create as broad a blocking surface as possible. In this situation, the blocker tries to catch the rusher in the "V" of his neck and flipper. The primary objective is to press the block of that "V" up into the rusher and continue driving to the sideline. If the pass rusher tries to disengage by reversing out underneath the seal to gain an inside rush lane, the blocker immediately whips his legs around and reverse crabs the defender. As soon as the blocker feels he is losing the rusher underneath while sealing, he should whip his legs around to reverse crab block.

If he begins to lose his rusher to the inside, he should also execute this same technique of seal blocking and possible reverse crab blocking, except that the seal block attempts to ride the rusher across the center of the formation and out toward the opposite sideline. Seal blocking, however, is used only after the back realizes he can no longer maintain the initial press of his pass-pro block and is losing his defender to the inside or outside.

If the pass-pro blocker realizes he is being overpowered by the pass rusher, the blocker immediately whips down into a cut-down block and scrambles into the defender's legs or rolls into the defender in order to maintain a blocking press. In this way, he will prevent the rusher from getting up and continuing his rush on the quarterback.

An important concept to understand is that the action of locking out the arms is often impossible to carry out. On the contrary, a blocking back will often find that he is locked onto a pass rusher after he has delivered a pass-pro blocking blow, meaning that he is pressed into the defender with a press of the palms, the forearms, and the chest as he attempts to maintain his blocking position between the rusher and the quarterback. The blocker's emphasis is now to maintain his press, staying in front of the rusher with an inside-out attitude and keeping a good foot base. The key is to maintain a good knee bend in order to enable the usually smaller pass-pro back to stay underneath the rusher and maintain good pass-pro leverage.

PASS-PRO BLOCKING A BLITZING LINEBACKER

When the back is assigned to pass block a linebacker, three techniques can be utilized. First, the back can carry out a normal pass-pro action in which he sets up in the linebacker's rush path as he blitzes. Since he is forced, however, to take the blitzing linebacker head on, he loses the advantage of an inside-out position and the ability to ride the pass rusher to the sideline. An effort to position himself inside-out on a blitzing linebacker just "opens the door" for the linebacker to get to the quarterback, given the linebacker's pursuit angle advantage. Therefore, the blocking back using the pass-pro technique against a blitzing linebacker is forced to take on a square stance and aim his block down the middle of the defender.

The better technique to use against the blitzing linebacker is simply to isolation block the linebacker before he can get through the line of scrimmage. The linebacker's rush lane is narrowest at the line of scrimmage due to the blocking and rushing action of the offensive and defensive linemen. This situation gives the blocking back the best opportunity to attack the blitzing linebacker and deliver a violent isolation-type block up under the linebacker's shoulder pads. As in the usual isolation block technique, the blocking back concentrates more on the initial contact than on any follow-through technique in an effort to stop the linebacker and stand him up. After the initial contact, the blocker attempts to stay pressed to the blitzer to create a pile-up at the line of scrimmage with the rest of the blockers and the rushers.

As was previously discussed, if the blitzing linebacker is able to clear the line of scrimmage, the blocking back will usually be at a strong disadvantage due to the "head of steam" that the linebacker will have on his blitz. In this situation, the blocker should execute a cut-down block by securing a tight fit down through the crotch of the blitzing linebacker. After executing the cut-down block, he must carry out his normal rolling follow-through action to prevent the linebacker from getting up to continue his rush on the quarterback.

BACKFIELD PASS BLOCKING TECHNIQUES AND PRACTICE DRILLS

The backs are almost always pressed for time in practice, because of their heavy assignment and execution loads—ballcarrying, faking, blocking, receiving, etc. Since pass blocking is often the toughest backfield blocking technique to master, a proper amount of practice time is needed. If the coach examines his practice format, he will see that more opportunities exist than he realizes to practice pass blocking and, for that matter, blocking in general. For example, during a skeleton pass scrimmage, no reason exists why a manager can't hold a cut-down dummy, 24 inches high, at the end of the tape, as shown in Diagram 12-6, so that the backs assigned to cut-down block the end defender on the line of scrimmage on a sprint-out pass play can practice their technique. The same concept could be utilized to enable a back who is pass-pro blocking practice against a pass rush by involving an extra player in the defensive end spot put on a pass rush with a large shield.

One of the greatest misconceptions coaches have is that blocking practice must be done "live," or at nearly full speed. Actually, the opposite is true. Much of good blocking is proper technique that can be practiced effectively through the concept of form blocking in which proper technique is emphasized rather than high speed "live" work. It is difficult for a player to develop a high degree of proficiency at a psychomotor skill by attempting to go full speed (i.e., emphasizing an aggressive attack), if he has not first mastered the fundamentals of that action.

Form blocking at half to three-quarter speed forces the back to concentrate on precise technique, and allows easier monitoring of the degree of precision attained by the back by both the coach and the player himself. During form blocking, all techniques of the skills are exaggerated to help the individual concentrate on each technique. Form blocking can be practiced all through unit and team practice. A thud scrimmage in which a back attacks the defender he is to block, slows down as he approaches the defender, and then stops is one of the biggest wastes of practice time. Certainly, the coach may not want excessive cut-down blocking action on the practice field for fear of injuries, but no good reason exists as to why the back who is assigned the cut-down block can't practice an explosive take-off, a proper outside-in approach on the outside knee of the defender, proper throttle-down action to drop his tail and maintain a proper base, and an explosive north-south ripping action of the cut-down block with a slow-motion ripping-up action of the inside arm north-south through the upper torso of the defender, thereby avoiding the dangerous full-speed cut-down blocking action. Thus, all the actual movements of the cut-down block can be practiced with a high degree of concentration and proficiency. This method is far superior to approaching the defender, stopping, and putting a hand on him to signify you have him. Remember, such form blocking emphasis is by no means limited to pass blocking.

Drill #1: Cut-Down

This drill simply practices an explosive take-off, proper outside-in positioning, proper throttling-down action, and the proper north-south ripping action of the cut-down block on a 24-inch high cut-down bag. Such a special low bag plays an important role in helping develop the low contact point just above the defender's knee. The backs must practice the cut-down block to both sides, as shown in Diagram 12-6.

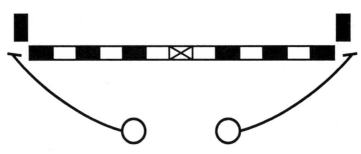

Diagram 12-6
Cut-down block drill.

Coaching Points: The person holding the bag must stand to the outside so he can avoid the cut-down blocker's action. It is important to emphasize the rolling, follow-through action after the contact of the cut-down block. Two blockers, as shown in Diagram 12-6, could easily go at the same time to produce maximum repetitions. As previously mentioned, this drill could be added to another drill, such as the skeleton pass drill, to help create extra cut-down blocking practice without extra practice time. It is also important to note that this same drill can be utilized to practice such run blocks as the lead block on an end-of-the-line defender, since the technique is quite similar.

Drill #2: Big Bertha

"Big Bertha" is the name given to the monstrous-sized pass blocking dummy hung from a frame. In the drill, a back simply takes a normal stance on a 45-degree angle from Bertha, steps up as on a normal pass pro blocking action to square up on Bertha, and practices the normal delivery of the pass-pro block. The blocker continues to rip up and press into Bertha until the coach blows the whistle. Big Bertha is shown in Diagram 12-7.

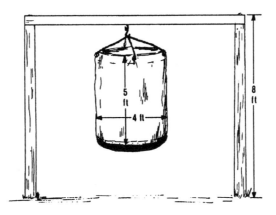

Diagram 12-7
Big Bertha

Coaching Points: All the techniques of a proper pass-pro block are stressed. Special emphasis is placed on snapping the hips under on delivery of the blow and maintaining proper press action.

Drill #3: Pass Pro Position

The pass-pro position drill emphasizes the blocking back's proper body positioning in his setup, his positioning on the rusher as he rushes, and his repositioning as he presses the block. Such proper positioning forces the rusher to rush through the back's outside shoulder. The drill is performed at three-quarter speed with little contact. It is similar to a mirror-type drill in which the blocker continually tries to maintain the proper positioning on the defender. The rushing defender utilizes sharp cuts, redirection of movement, and changes of speed, in an attempt to force the blocker out of proper position and open a better rushing lane to the quarter-back. The back continually readjusts his positioning to maintain the desired position. This action is shown in Diagram 12-8.

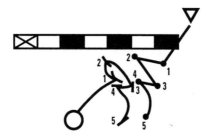

Diagram 12-8
Pass-pro position drill.

Coaching Points: The coach continually watches to see if the blocker is forcing the rusher to rush through his outside shoulder. The coach checks for such proper techniques as foot shuffle (not crossing the feet), maintaining a low, compact base, proper action for the delivery of the blow (although in a modified sense, this is a three-quarter speed drill), and proper lateral sliding action as the blocker reacts to the movement of the rusher. Again, the focus of both this drill and the technique is to keep the blocker's body between the rusher and the quarterback, thereby forcing the rusher to rush through the blocking back's outside shoulder.

Drill #4: Pass Pro

The pass-pro drill is simply simulation of a back executing his pass-pro blocking techniques against the various rushing techniques of a defensive end, an outside linebacker, or an inside linebacker. The defender varies his techniques. Two sets of rushers and blockers can drill at the same time if they are spaced far enough apart to avoid unnecessary collisions (refer to Diagram 12-9).

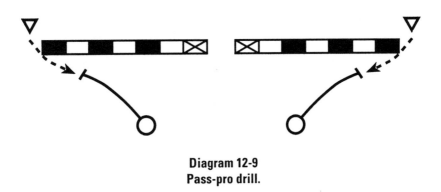

Diagram 12-9
Pass-pro drill.

Coaching Points: Diagram 12-9 shows the use of two tapes, or hoses, so that two sets of rushers-blockers are adequately spaced to avoid interfering with each other while performing the drill. The coach, of course, is teaching all the various techniques associated with the pass-pro blocking skills.

Drill #5: Pass-Pro, Cut-Down, Kick-Out

This drill is set up the same as the pass-pro drill that is shown in Diagram 12-8. The back, however, practices the variety of his end-of-the-line blocking techniques—pass-pro, cut-down, and kick-out—against a variety of defensive reactions. This drill is perhaps more realistic than the pass-pro drill, since it creates a more game-like situation and prevents the defender from uncommonly teeing off in an abnormally explosive pass rush.

Coaching Points: Again, the cut-down block can be practiced for both pass and run blocking assignments.

Drill #6: Ride-In/Ride-Out

This drill is actually an important isolated segment of the pass-pro blocking technique—avoiding losing a rusher to the inside or outside. In this situation, the blocker develops the proper techniques for riding the defender out to the sideline or across the formation to the opposite sideline by driving his head up in front of the defender to execute a seal block technique. The drill is set up by having a defender stand directly in front of the blocking back. The blocker presses up against the rusher. On a signal, the rusher blows past the blocker to the inside or the outside to simulate the situation of the back losing the rusher. The blocking back now executes his proper seal blocking techniques to ride the rusher out to the sideline or across the formation toward the opposite sideline, as shown in Diagram 12-10.

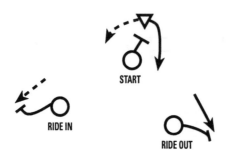

Diagram 12-10
Ride-in/ride-out drill.

Coaching Points: The coach can enhance the value of the drill by having the rusher attempt to reverse (spin) out under the seal blocking technique to force the back to execute proper scramble blocking techniques.

Drill #7: Scramble Block

The scramble block is a last ditch effort when no other technique can be utilized. It is, however, a very effective technique to keep the rusher from the quarterback. The scramble block drill helps develop the pass-pro back's ability to scramble block the rusher from an unsettled and off-balance position. It is set up by having the pass-pro blocker assume the unorthodox leaning position against a rusher, as seen in the left photo of Figure 12-3. On the coach's signal, the rusher breaks away from the leaning back to cause him to lose his balance and fall forward, thereby creating a simulation of the typical unsettled, off-balance situation of a pass-pro blocking back losing his defender and being in an awkward position. The back must immediately go into a scramble block by attempting to scramble up tightly into the rusher's legs, as illustrated in Figure 12-4. He continues the scramble action until the whistle is blown.

Coaching Point: The coach must concentrate on getting the backs to maintain a press of the scramble block up into the legs of the rusher until the whistle is blown.

Starting position block   **Rusher breaking away**

**Figure 12-3
Scramble block drill.**

**Figure 12-4
Application of scramble.**

215

THE AUTHOR

Steve Axman is the head football coach at Northern Arizona University. In his seven seasons at the helm of the NAU football program, Axman has led the Lumberjacks to national prominence. The 1996 season was highlighted by NAU's first-ever appearance in the Division I-AA post-season tournament. In addition, NAU became the first college team—at any level—to have both a 2,000-yard rusher (Archie Amerson) and a 3,000-yard passer (Travis Brown) in a single season.

Prior to assuming his present position in 1990, Axman was on the coaching staff at the University of Maryland, where he coached the quarterbacks—most notably New York Jet signal-caller Neil O'Donnell. Before his stint in Maryland, Axman served as the offensive coordinator at UCLA from 1987 to 1988. During his tenure on the Bruins' staff, Axman coached the quarterbacks—one of whom was NFL great Troy Aikman of the Dallas Cowboys. A 1969 graduate of C.W. Post College, Axman has also held positions on the gridiron staffs of Standford University, the Denver Gold (USFL), the University of Arizona, the University of Illinois, the U.S. Military Academy, Albany State University, and East Stroudsburg State University.

Axman is widely renowned as having one of the most creative offensive minds in the game. An accomplished writer, he has authored several books and articles on football schemes, techniques and strategies.

Axman and his wife, Dr. Marie Axman, reside in Flagstaff, Arizona. The Axmans have four daughters—Mary Beth, Jaclyn, Melissa and Kimberly.